T0286791

Cambridge Elements ≡

Elements in Bioethics and Neuroethics
edited by
Thomasine Kushner
California Pacific Medical Center, San Francisco

IMMUNE ETHICS

Walter Glannon

CAMBRIDGE
UNIVERSITY PRESS

CAMBRIDGE
UNIVERSITY PRESS

Shaftesbury Road, Cambridge CB2 8EA, United Kingdom

One Liberty Plaza, 20th Floor, New York, NY 10006, USA

477 Williamstown Road, Port Melbourne, VIC 3207, Australia

314–321, 3rd Floor, Plot 3, Splendor Forum, Jasola District Centre,
New Delhi – 110025, India

103 Penang Road, #05–06/07, Visioncrest Commercial, Singapore 238467

Cambridge University Press is part of Cambridge University Press & Assessment,
a department of the University of Cambridge.

We share the University's mission to contribute to society through the pursuit of
education, learning and research at the highest international levels of excellence.

www.cambridge.org
Information on this title: www.cambridge.org/9781009304597

DOI: 10.1017/9781009304610

First published 2023

A catalogue record for this publication is available from the British Library.

ISBN 978-1-009-30459-7 Paperback
ISSN 2752-3934 (online)
ISSN 2752-3926 (print)

Cambridge University Press & Assessment has no responsibility for the persistence or
accuracy of URLs for external or third-party internet websites referred to in this
publication and does not guarantee that any content on such websites is, or will
remain, accurate or appropriate.

Immune Ethics

Elements in Bioethics and Neuroethics

DOI: 10.1017/9781009304610
First published online: July 2023

Walter Glannon

Author for correspondence: Walter Glannon, wglannon@ucalgary.ca

Abstract: The immune system maintains homeostasis within human organisms and protects them from pathogenic threats. But sometimes it cannot provide this protection on its own, and vaccines may be necessary to ensure our health and survival. Immune functions can become dysregulated and result in autoimmune disease or multi-system damage. Pharmacological and genomic interventions may activate or modulate immune functions to prevent these outcomes. This Element is an analysis and discussion of some of the ethical implications of these interventions. After describing the main components of innate and adaptive immunity and how it might be enhanced, it considers the potential benefit and harm from vaccines against addiction and viruses, immunotherapy for cancer, neuro-immunomodulating agents to prevent or treat neurodevelopmental and neurodegenerative diseases, and gene editing of immunity to enable xenotransplantation and prevent infectious disease. The Element concludes with an exploration of a possible outcome of natural competition between humans and microbes.

Keywords: adaptive immunity, antigens, benefit, harm, innate immunity, microbes, pathogens, vaccines, viruses, xenotransplantation

ISBNs: 9781009304597 (PB), 9781009304610 (OC)
ISSNs: 2752-3934 (online), 2752-3926 (print)

Contents

1 Introduction

Human survival depends on the immune system. The traditional view of immunity is that it is designed to defend human organisms against infectious agents.[1] But its functions include more than defense. Many bacteria, viruses, fungi, and other microbes are not eliminated from the body but tolerated by the immune system and coexist with it in a symbiotic relationship.[2] Immune cells also have a critical role in cell development, tissue repair, wound healing, and elimination of debris from naturally programmed cell death.[3] The immune system does not function independently of the central nervous and other bodily systems but interacts with them in salutary or deleterious ways. Distinguishing between what is internal to the immune system and what is external to it does not explain why some immune mechanisms protect organisms or why others threaten them. Innate and adaptive immunity have evolved not only to protect us from external threats but also to maintain equilibrium within the organism.[4] The immune system's properties of defense, development, tolerance, control, maintenance, repair, and elimination enable us to adapt to and survive in the world we share with microbes.[5]

There are limitations to the immune system's natural ability to protect us from pathogens and maintain homeostasis. This is the organism's ability to regulate its internal milieu and preserve functional equilibrium. The Black Death of 1346–50 caused by the bacterium *Yersinia pestis* reduced the population in Europe, the Middle East, and Northern Africa by 30–50 percent.[6] This was the same bacterium responsible for the earlier Plague of Justinian around CE 541. Improvements in hygiene, infrastructure, and our understanding of our relationship to the environment have prevented similar bacterial pandemics. Yet morbidity and mortality from viruses and cancer underscore the limitations of immunity's protective function. Antibiotics, vaccines, and antiviral and antifungal drugs activate immune mechanisms to prevent or neutralize microbial threats to us.

But some of these threats may evade these interventions and harm us by causing disability and death. Cancer cells may disable innate and adaptive cells and proteins necessary for homeostasis and eventually lead to these same harmful outcomes. In some circumstances, components of the immune system itself, rather than pathogens, cause it to become dysfunctional. Autoreactive antibodies directed against self-antigens have been implicated in the pathogenesis of autoimmune diseases that destroy healthy cells, tissues, and organs. Proliferation of pro-inflammatory cells and proteins in response to viral infections can induce excess inflammation resulting in multi-organ failure and contribute to neurodevelopmental and neurodegenerative disorders.

It may be possible to overcome some of these limitations. Gene editing could make us and future generations less susceptible to viruses. Immune-based therapies using monoclonal antibodies can activate T cells to neutralize and destroy cancer cells. Tolerogenic drugs could prevent some components of the immune system from attacking others and reduce the incidence of autoimmune disease. They could also modulate inflammatory mechanisms in the brain and thereby prevent or mitigate the effects of neuropsychiatric disorders. These same drugs could prevent rejection of allografts transplanted from one human to another and xenografts transplanted from animals to humans.

These and other actual and possible interventions in the immune system raise ethical questions. They include: In what sense can immune functions be enhanced, and how would enhancing them benefit us? Is there a moral obligation for adults to be vaccinated against certain viruses, and to have their children vaccinated? Could refusing vaccination justifiably limit one's access to medical care? Do the therapeutic effects of immunotherapy for cancer always outweigh the actual and potentially harmful effects? Would the use of gene editing to induce immune tolerance of transplanted tissues and organs compromise protective immunity and make transplant recipients susceptible to opportunistic infections? Should researchers open the blood-brain barrier to infuse drugs into the brain to prevent or control neurodevelopmental and neurodegenerative diseases? Could this be done without altering normal neuronal processes? Should we edit genes at the germline to prevent future people from being infected by viruses or other pathogens ? Would it be bad if humans lost in competition with pathogens for survival and became extinct? All these questions regard different aspects in which humans can benefit from or be harmed by natural defects or limitations in the immune system and by attempts to intervene, or failing to intervene, in it. How one responds to these ethical questions must be informed by the cellular and molecular mechanisms of innate and adaptive immunity. This Element is an analysis and discussion of these questions.

Many philosophers use "ethics" and "morality" interchangeably in making normative judgments about actions and policies. I follow that practice here in assessing how immune function and dysfunction, and interventions to alter it, can affect persons in positive and negative ways. Although there are differences in the original meaning of these terms, they are not normatively significant. Ethics and morality both consider the rights, needs, and interests of individuals and groups, how they make claims on others, whether or how others meet these claims, and how actions and consequences that realize or defeat these claims can benefit or harm them. One benefits when an action realizes an interest one has in a certain state of affairs. One is harmed when an action defeats this interest. An action benefits a person when it makes them better off in some respect and harms them when it makes them worse off.[7] Explicitly or implicitly, I use deontological, consequentialist, nonconsequentialist, and contractualist theories to assess normative claims about different interventions in the immune system. Deontological theories focus on actions that prioritize rights, autonomy, and duties over consequences.[8] Consequentialist theories focus on actions that bring about the best consequences.[9] Nonconsequentialist theories do not deny the normative significance of good outcomes but hold that there is no moral obligation to maximize them.[10] Contractualist theories focus on principles of action based on mutual interest and respect that no one could reasonably reject.[11]

In Section 2, I describe the main components of the immune system to establish an empirical framework within which to discuss the ethical implications of interventions to change it. I analyze and discuss whether or to what extent the immune system can be enhanced in Section 3. The most plausible conception of immune enhancement is not one of increasing circulating levels of immune cells and proteins but one that generates and maintains them at optimal levels to eliminate life-threatening antigens while tolerating non-life-threatening antigens. An enhanced immune system is one in which immunogenicity is balanced with immune tolerance. There is an equilibrium between activating and inhibitory immune cells and molecules. Interventions intended to improve or maintain immune function must ensure this equilibrium. Vaccines designed to activate B and T cells and antibodies against pathogens, as well as immunotherapy for cancer, are examples of immunogenic mechanisms. Drugs designed to prevent the production of autoreactive lymphocytes implicated in autoimmune diseases, as well as to prevent hyperacute rejection of transplanted organs from humans or nonhuman animals, are examples of tolerogenic mechanisms.

In Section 4, I discuss ethical issues surrounding vaccines. I consider some of the promises and pitfalls of developing and using vaccines to prevent or treat addictions. These issues must be framed by the social context in which addiction occurs and the view that addiction is to some extent learned behavior. I also consider questions about the justification of challenge trials involving healthy human subjects to test the safety and efficacy of vaccines for viruses such as SARS-CoV-2 (COVID-19). In discussing vaccines to prevent infectious diseases, I argue that there is a general moral obligation for widespread vaccination against the measles virus. But there may not be a similar obligation for other viruses, and I describe some circumstances in which vaccination exemptions would be permissible. I also consider whether refusal to be vaccinated justifies restricting or denying access to certain types of medical care.

In Section 5, I discuss immunotherapy for cancer. While this type of therapy can stimulate production of T lymphocytes to attack cancer cells resistant to chemotherapy, in some cases they may trigger a hyperactive inflammatory response that could damage healthy cells, tissues, and organs. The efficacy of immunotherapy in killing cancer cells would not rule out a similar type of collateral damage resulting from chemotherapy. Immunotherapy may only be offered for a limited period of time, which can influence an assessment of its benefits. Moreover, this therapy may be a treatment of last resort when all other treatments have failed. This could influence a patient's emotional state and assessment of its benefits and risks. It may also raise questions about their capacity to give informed consent to undergo therapy.

I explore possible interventions in the brain to modulate neuroimmune interactions in Section 6. Microglia and cytokines are the critical immune components in these interactions. These interventions include neuromodulating agents that might prevent or reverse excess inflammatory and other pathogenic processes in the brain. These agents would have to target neuroimmune dysregulation with a high level of specificity and at the right stage of neurodevelopmental or neurodegenerative pathophysiology to modulate dysregulated neural functions while leaving normal neural functions intact. Among the ethical issues these interventions raise is whether it would be permissible to enroll individuals deemed at risk of developing a neurological or psychiatric disorder but who are asymptomatic in research to test their safety and efficacy.

In Section 7, I discuss the use of genetic engineering of the immune system to overcome allograft and xenograft rejection in tissue and organ transplantation. By targeting the genetic mechanisms at the source of graft rejection, gene editing may be more effective in promoting successful human-to-human and animal-to-human transplantation than tolerogenic drugs modulating natural molecular mechanisms. But it cannot be assumed that altering the immune system's recognition of foreign antigens from tissue would leave all other immune functions intact. I consider the possibility of germline gene editing to eliminate susceptibility to viruses. This requires discussion of the unknown possible long-term benefits and risks of using this technique in people who exist now and those who will exist in the future. I also consider somatic cell gene editing of immunity to treat certain diseases. While this technique does not entail the risk of transmitting unwanted adverse effects to offspring, as in germline editing, it may still entail some risk. In the final Section 8, I speculate on the possibility that humans and their immune systems could one day lose in the competition with life-threatening microbes and consider whether this would be good, bad, or morally neutral.

2 The Human Immune System

The immune system is a complex set of functions that normally overlap and interact in a coordinated way to maintain homeostasis within the organism and protect it from pathogens (Figure 1).[12] The evolutionarily older innate system is activated and responds generally and nonspecifically to microbes perceived as threats to destroy and clear them from the organism. The main components of the innate immune system are dendritic cells, macrophages, neutrophils, eosinophils, phagocytes, natural killer (NK) cells, and complement. This last component is a set of proteins that mediate immune functions such as inflammation, cell lysis (when the cell membrane ruptures and dies), and tagging microbes for phagocytosis (the engulfment of microbes for elimination). As the name implies, these proteins complement the action of other immune cells and molecules. This is one respect in which innate and adaptive systems interact. The function of phagocytes to present antigens to T and B lymphocytes is another.

The evolutionarily more recent adaptive immune system consists mainly of B and T cells (B and T lymphocytes) in the tissue between the body's cells, and antibodies in the blood and other bodily fluids. T cells are produced by the thymus gland, and B cells are produced in the bone marrow. Once they reach full maturity, these cells migrate to and reside in the lymph nodes and spleen. T cells are one type of cell that produces cytokines. These signaling protein molecules regulate immune cellular communication. Cytokines also mediate inflammatory responses to infectious agents. They include chemokines, interleukins, and interferons. Cells in both innate and adaptive immune systems produce cytokines.

Adaptive immunity is divided into humoral and cell-mediated types. Humoral immunity (from the idea of bodily "humors") consists of antibodies,

Innate immune system	Adaptive immune system
Dendritic cells	T cells (T lymphocytes, e.g., CD4+, CD8+)
Macrophages	B cells (B lymphocytes)
Neutrophils	Antibodies: antigen-specific, produced by B cells
Eosinophils	Cytokines released by adaptive immune
Phagocytes	cells, especially helper T cells
Natural killer (NK) cells	
Complement	
Cytokines (chemokines, interferons, interleukins) released by innate immune cells	

Figure 1 The human immune system: main components

which are immunoglobin molecules activated in response to an antigen. B cells contribute to humoral immunity by producing antibodies. There are five types of immunoglobins: IgG, IgM, IgA, IgD, and IgE. They circulate in the blood and on cell surfaces. An antigen is any biological entity that combines with antibodies and triggers their response to it. Antigens may be from sources external or internal to the body. They may be present on microbes such as bacteria, viruses, fungi, tissue in transplanted organs, and cancer cells. An antigenic epitope is the smallest identifiable part of an antigen with which an antibody specifically interacts. "In general, the more complex the antigen, the more stimulatory or immunogenic it will be in eliciting an immune response."[13] As I explain in the next section, "immunogenic" may refer to both positive and negative effects in the organism and beneficial and harmful effects in persons. This depends on the type and level of immune response that an epitope elicits.

Cell-mediated immunity consists mainly of mature T cells. They interact with cytokines released in response to an antigen, as well as with macrophages and phagocytes. T cells do not produce antibodies but regulate B cell responses to antigens. Effector B and T cells activate a range of immune functions. Cell-mediated immunity does not rely on antibodies. CD4+ and CD8+ cells are two types of T lymphocytes in antigen-specific activation. The first type, also called "helper T cells," produce cytokines. The second type, also called "cytotoxic T cells," produce cytokines as well and initiate a process resulting in cell death. Effector B and T lymphocytes stimulate the production of other immune cells. In addition to mediating B cell functions, regulatory T lymphocytes down-regulate overactive immune processes and thereby promote immune tolerance of certain foreign and self-antigens. Another key factor in immunity is the major histocompatibility complex (MHC). This is a collection of genes controlling different immune functions. The MHC regulates T cell responses to foreign tissue antigens as well as T cell autorecognition. Human leukocyte antigen (HLA) is the human version of MHC. HLA has a critical role in immune surveillance and the immune response to transplanted solid organs and tissues.

The hallmark of the adaptive system is immunological memory. B and T cells that have encountered an antigen can respond more effectively in subsequent encounters with it than innate immune cells and proteins. For this reason, they are described as memory B and T cells. In contrast to the generalized, nonspecific rapid response of the innate system to an infectious agent, the more specific response of the adaptive system may take days or even weeks to occur as it forms a memory of the antigen following an initial encounter with it. Like antibodies, B and T lymphocytes are antigen-specific. This enables an adaptive response that targets a particular perceived threat to the organism.

The success or failure of an adaptive response to a pathogen depends on whether, or to what extent, antibodies and memory B and T cells recognize the antigen it expresses after an initial exposure. The ability of immunological memory to protect us from pathogens may be limited by the fact that most antigens contain a variety of epitopes, and activation of antibodies and effector T cells may vary depending on different receptors for different antigen epitopes. How antibodies and cells respond may be influenced by *antigenic drift* and *antigenic shift*.[14] The first refers to the process in which there is an accumulation of genetic errors during viral replication. The second refers to the process in which recombination causes changes in the dominant antigen expressed by a virus. These processes influence *antigenic variation,* the mechanism by which a protozoan, bacterium, or virus evolves by altering the proteins on its surface to avoid a host immune response. This can impair the ability of vaccines to control them because they cannot target a specific antigen. It may promote *antigenic sin.*[15] This refers to the immune system's tendency to preferentially respond to an antigen from a previous infection when a second slightly different version of the antigen is encountered. The response depends on the organism's immune history.

Antigenic sin is one hypothesis for the high mortality rate among young adults during the 1918 influenza pandemic. They were probably exposed to the H3N8 influenza strain when they were born around 1889–1890. This exposure may have "primed" their immune systems to respond to the antigen from this virus instead of to the antigen (epitope) from the H1N1 virus of 1918. The "sin" was the immune system's failure to recognize and respond to the more immediate and virulent pathogenic threat. In proposing this hypothesis, Alain Gagnon and coauthors explain that "developing immunological memory to an antigenically dissimilar subtype in early life may actually subvert the immune system, thereby increasing the risk of death when the individual is infected by a novel strain later in life."[16] The older memory was the predominant memory controlling the response to the H1N1 epitope. Older adults did not have the same rate of mortality as younger adults probably because of immunologic cross-protection from earlier exposure to the virus that was circulating in the population before the 1889–1890 influenza pandemic. "One mechanistic explanation for this is that conserved, but non-neutralizing epitopes, on the secondary viruses elicit a memory antibody response generated during the first infection that is faster and greater in magnitude than the *de novo* response, but not protective against the new strain. As a result, these memory cells essentially out-compete the protective cells that would normally be newly generated against the subsequent exposures."[17]

Innate and adaptive immunity interact in many ways. Complement in the innate system interacts with cytokines in the adaptive systems in mediating inflammation. Macrophages in the innate system activate and interact with B and T lymphocytes that target antigens. The memory of the antigen in these lymphocytes induces a more vigorous response to it. Lymphocytes also recruit other cells and soluble proteins to remove microbes from the body. In addition, cytokines continue inflammatory processes initiated by macrophages and complement to destroy pathogens. These interactions may complicate interventions designed to improve specific immune functions. Altering some functions may also alter others in ways that may not always be salutary or benign.

The idea that the immune system has evolved to protect the organism from microbial threats previously led some researchers to draw a "self-nonself" distinction in immunology.[18] Endogenous cells and proteins (self) protect the organism; exogenous agents (nonself) threaten it. But more recent research has shown that whether these molecules are internal or external to the organism does not determine whether they promote health or disease. Rather, what determines this is whether they maintain or disrupt homeostasis.

Foreign antigens on bacteria, fungi, and other microbes may be tolerated rather than rejected to preserve functional equilibrium. The body's own immune cells can disrupt it in different forms of pathological autoreactivity. This may occur from molecular mimicry.[19] When the immune system encounters an infectious agent, there may be a cross-reactive immune response to a self-antigen that is molecularly similar to a foreign antigen expressed by a pathogen. This similarity can cause T cells to mistake one antigen for the other and direct antibodies to attack and destroy the infected individual's own healthy cells. This is one explanation for the pathogenesis of autoimmune diseases such as type 1 diabetes, where autoreactive lymphocytes and autoantibodies attack and destroy pancreatic islet cells that produce insulin. There is cross-reactivity between B and T cells and molecular fragments of the coxsackie virus and cytomegalovirus, which can cause these cells and antibodies to become autoreactive. Cross-reactivity and the inflammatory response it elicits might also partly explain the destruction of myelin (the sheath that insulates nerve cell axons that conduct electrical impulses in the brain) in multiple sclerosis.

Pro-inflammatory cytokines are necessary to destroy infectious agents. But chronic hypersecretion of these signaling protein molecules can damage healthy tissues and organs. These "cytokine storms," or "cytokine release syndromes," are "life-threatening systemic inflammatory syndromes involving elevated levels of circulating cytokines and immune cell hyperactivation that can be triggered by various therapies, pathogens, cancers, autoimmune conditions, and monogenic disorders."[20] They have been cited as one explanation for the high mortality rate from pulmonary inflammation and lung damage among young adults in the 1918 influenza pandemic and older adults in the first two waves of the SARS-CoV-2 pandemic in 2020 and 2021.

Autoimmune diseases and cytokine release syndrome illustrate that the immune system's own cells and molecules do not always promote the health and survival of the organism. Pharmacological attempts to induce innate and adaptive tolerance rather than elimination of non-life-threatening viral antigens and antigens on transplanted tissue to prevent graft rejection are examples that blur the distinction between self and nonself. Passive transfer of the immunoglobin IgG across the placenta during pregnancy is an example of natural immune tolerance of foreign antigens. Another example is gut microbiota and other microbes in the body that have a symbiotic relationship with immune functions. They contribute to cell development, tissue repair, and eliminate debris from cell death in their interaction with neutrophils and macrophages.

Whether immunity is regulated or dysregulated depends on how innate and adaptive systems respond, or fail to respond, to different antigens in destroying or tolerating them. While destructive responses to life-threatening antigens seem to support a distinction between the immune self and nonself, tolerance of other antigens suggests that there is a continuum from one to the other. Destruction and tolerance are not programmed into immune functions but depend on how the immune system perceives antigens and other molecules in different biological circumstances. "Immune defense and pathogenicity are not intrinsic properties of host and microbes. Rather, they are a matter of evolutionary and ecological context."[21] In some contexts, tolerating an antigen can promote adaptability and survival of the organism. In others, eliminating the antigen is the only way to achieve these goals.

Thomas Pradeu outlines two main problems with the self-nonself theory of immunity:

> First, far from being always pathological, autoimmunity has been proved to be a necessary component of everyday immunity. A degree of autoreactivity (ie., a reaction to "self") characterizes the lymphocytes generated and selected in primary lymphoid organs as well as naive lymphocytes always circulating in the periphery ... Effector T cells are selected only if they react weakly to self elements (and not if they do not react at all). There exists in fact a continuum from autoreactivity (interactions between immune receptors and endogenous motifs) and to autoimmunity (the triggering of an effector response targeting endogenous motifs) and to autoimmune diseases (only the latter situation is pathological ...) it consists in the destruction of endogenous components, in a sustained manner and on a large scale – a given organ or even the whole organism in the case of systemic autoimmune diseases such as lupus.[22]

Second, many genetically foreign entities are not eliminated by the immune system and are instead actively tolerated via regulatory immune responses. This includes examples such as foeto-maternal tolerance and various forms of chimerism, but also, and most crucially, immunological tolerance to a large number of bacteria, archaea, viruses, and fungi at all of the body's interfaces, including the gut, skin, lungs, sexual organs, and so on . . . Immunological interactions between host and microbes enable, in general, a peaceful coexistence between these two partners.[23]

Pradeu concludes: "The upshot is that the self-nonself theory is inadequate or at least incomplete because many self components trigger immune responses and many nonself components are actively tolerated by the immune system."[24]

The identity of an organism does not exclude but includes microbes. In many circumstances, however, tolerance of and coexistence with certain microbes are not compatible with the organism's survival. Some antigens can overwhelm the immune system and lead to the organism's demise. Innate and adaptive immunity must not tolerate but eliminate them. Again, though, whether tolerance or elimination is most conducive to survival does not depend on whether a biological entity is endogenous or exogenous to the organism. Rather, it depends on whether an antigen poses a threat to the organism and how different components of the immune system respond to the antigen.

3 Can the Immune System Be Enhanced?

Some bioethicists have discussed the idea of enhancing immunity.[25] Typically these are general claims about how genetic manipulation could improve immune functions without much detail about how this would occur. Immunologists and scientists in related fields often use "augment," "boost," and "enhance" interchangeably. The general idea of enhancement suggests interventions in the immune system that would provide more protection against infectious agents than what it naturally provides. It also suggests interventions that would prevent it from turning against itself.

"Enhancement" has been defined by bioethicists and philosophers as any intervention "designed to improve human form or functioning beyond what is necessary to sustain or restore good health."[26] "Therapy" can be described as any intervention that restores or maintains good health. This may include preventive measures. Some argue that there is no clear distinction between enhancement and therapy. John Harris claims that "treatments or preventive measures which protect humans from things to which they are normally vulnerable, or which prevent harm . . . are necessarily also enhancements."[27] It is unclear whether any intervention designed to improve the immune system could do more than maintain homeostasis and protect the organism from microbial threats. In this regard, there may be no strict distinction between enhancement, therapy, and prevention for interventions in the immune system.

Vaccines stimulate the production of B and T cells and neutralizing antibodies against viral antigens to prevent us from being infected by them. The use of monoclonal antibodies to activate T cells and destroy cancer cells in immuno-oncology is intended to prevent these cells from proliferating uncontrollably and killing us. These immunogenic interventions may control bacterial, viral, and other infections more effectively than NK cells, B and T lymphocytes, antibodies, and other immune cells and molecules naturally responding to antigens on their own.

But simply increasing the number of immune cells or proteins does not always maintain homeostasis, promote health, and prevent disease. Any plausible sense of enhancing immunity must be optimizing rather than maximizing.[28] This would mean maintaining optimal levels of immunogenic and tolerogenic processes. Chronic hyperactivation of pro-inflammatory cytokines in response to a pathogen can cause collateral damage to healthy cells, tissues, and organs. A higher number of autoreactive B cells and autoantibodies that mistake self-antigens for foreign antigens and attack healthy cells can result in autoimmune disease. Increased activation of any component of the immune system must be within optimal levels to maintain homeostasis and protect the organism from external threats. In infectious diseases requiring an initial vaccine and subsequent boosters, the number and timing of vaccinations are critical to optimizing production of neutralizing antibodies against a pathogen. Administering multiple vaccines over a relatively brief period could inhibit antibody production and increase rather than decrease susceptibility to a disease. There are limits to the extent to which levels of immune cells and molecules can be increased without inducing uncontrolled cell proliferation resulting in various cancers or organ failure. Interventions must promote and maintain balance between activating and inhibiting immune functions.

Any intervention designed to optimize the immune response to an infectious agent must ensure that the response is proportional to the threat it poses to the organism. Otherwise, it can do more harm to an infected person than the agent itself. In some cases, the natural balance between activating and inhibiting immune responses to antigens may not hold. In their discussion of cytokine storms, David Fajgenbaum and Carl June point out that "the line between a normal and a dysregulated response to a severe infection is blurry, especially considering that certain cytokines may be both helpful in controlling an infection and harmful to the host."[29] Innate- and adaptive-induced inflammation is necessary to neutralize and eliminate pathogens from the body without damaging the body's own healthy cells and tissues. Referring to pro- and anti-inflammatory cytokines, the authors state that "the interdependence of these inflammatory mediators further complicates the distinction between a normal and dysregulated response."[30] Attempts to optimize immune function must recognize this and other forms of interdependence between and among different components of immunity.

Questions about enhancement pertain not only to immunogenicity but to immune tolerance as well. The ability of the immune system to tolerate some antigens may be as important as the ability to eliminate others. Tolerance refers to the absence of destruction of cells and molecules by the immune system.[31] The tolerance of antibodies crossing the placenta during pregnancy is one example. In addition, tolerogenic drugs modulating responses to foreign antigens from non-life-threatening viruses, such as herpes simplex, might prevent or reduce chronic inflammation in the brain and thereby reduce the risk of dementia and other neuropsychiatric disorders. This same class of drugs could modulate the immune response to HLA in transplanted tissues and organs and allow the body to accept rather than reject them. They could also modulate B and T cell reactions to self molecules and tissues implicated in autoimmune disease. By stimulating tolerogenic mechanisms, these and other pharmacological interventions could optimize immune functions in promoting health and preventing disease.

The fact that immune functions may be in varying states of equilibrium or disequilibrium complicates the question of the extent to which interventions could correct immune dysregulation and regulate responses to foreign and self-antigens. Theoretically, drugs designed to modulate the production of cytokines from CD4+ and CD8+ T cells could prevent cytokine release syndrome. But too much inhibition of pro-inflammatory cytokines could weaken the inflammatory response necessary to destroy pathogens invading the body. Tolerogenic drugs for transplant recipients may not make them as vulnerable to infection and cancer as they would be from immunosuppressive drugs. But if they inhibited B and T lymphocyte production, then they could make one susceptible to opportunistic infections. Immunogenic drugs could control cancer by activating effector T cells and blocking tumor cell proliferation. Yet they could also "lead to autoimmune syndromes, underscoring the delicate balance between breaking tolerance to treat tumors and altering immune homeostasis systemically."[32] So, even modulated immune responses may involve trade-offs in benefiting people in some respects and potentially harming them in others. Researchers and patients must weigh these trade-offs in prescribing and consenting to interventions that at best may promote less than optimal overall immune function.

One possible form of optimizing immune responses to antigens would be the use of immunomodulating drugs to balance activating, pro-inflammatory cytokines such as interleukin-1 (IL-1), interkeukin-6 (IL-6), and tumor necrosis factor-alpha (TNF-a), and inhibiting, anti-inflammatory cytokines such as inter-leukin 4 (IL-4) and interleukin 10 (IL-10). This implicitly relies on a clear distinction between normal and dysregulated cytokine responses to antigens. Yet if, as Fajgenbaum and June claim, this distinction cannot clearly be drawn, then it is unclear whether an intervention designed to modulate cytokine activation and prevent cytokine proliferation would have this effect and thereby benefit and not harm the recipient. Given the interdependence of inflammatory mediators, it is possible that blocking or reducing circulating levels of pro-inflammatory cytokines could result in a level of inflammation inadequate to neutralize and eliminate pathogens from the body.

Modified autologous T cells have been used to treat tumors in some patients with leukemia, lymphoma, multiple myeloma, and melanoma.[33] Macrophages are the main regulators of T cell activation, and they can be recruited to activate T cells to destroy cancer cells driving tumor development and progression. But macrophages can either activate or inhibit T cells based on their phenotype.[34] An intervention designed to kill cancer cells would have to activate the right macrophage phenotype. Macrophages can also induce cytokine secretion and thus inflammation. Targeting macrophages or T cells to "turbocharge" them with drugs such as monoclonal antibodies, or "designer cytokines" in tumor necrosis factor-based therapies targeting tumor vasculature,[35] would require a high level of specificity in destroying cancer cells and preserving healthy cells. The intended salutary effects of these agents would depend on their interaction with myeloid cells, which can promote or block tumor progression. Given the interdependence of immune functions, it is unclear how selective these inter-ventions could be, and how they might benefit or harm human recipients.

Tolerogenic agents such as vitamin D3, retinoic acid, dexamethasone, and dendritic cell-targeted nanomedicines might modulate humoral and cellular reactions to self-antigens by limiting activation of autoreactive antibodies.[36] This might prevent the pathogenesis of autoimmune diseases. It would depend on the extent to which these agents could control antigenic mimicry and prevent these antibodies from attacking host cells. Still, this may involve genetic factors that they could not control. In their discussion of autoimmunity and tolerance, Thao Doan, Roger Melvold, and Carl Waltenbaugh point out that:

> Genetic factors that provide variation in the immune capacity of different individuals can also make some individuals more susceptible to developing autoimmunity than others. Several specific genes have been identified that are associated with increased risk of certain autoimmune diseases. In humans, several genes within the HLA complex have been found to occur more frequently among patients with specific autoimmune diseases …

Autoimmunity is therefore a complex situation with multiple mechanisms, multiple causes, and multiple modifying factors. But what all of these factors have in common is that they contribute to a breakdown in the immune system's ability to refrain from attacking self-antigens, in other words, a breakdown in self tolerance.[37]

These authors underscore the variability among people in their immune responses to foreign and self-antigens. "A given antigen may provoke different responses in different individuals. A molecule that is immunogenic for one person may be tolerogenic for another and perhaps unrecognized by a third person."[38] They cite four major factors that account for these differences:

The first is the genetic constitution of each individual. Several genes influence how our immune system responds to a given antigen, and these can differ considerably among individuals. The second factor is the physical state of the antigen ... The third factor is often related to therapeutic treatment, where application of chemical or physical agents (e.g., drugs or irradiation) can alter an individual's immune response. As a result, an antigen that was previously tolerogenic to that individual may subsequently be seen as immunogenic or vice versa ... Finally, all individuals have "holes" in their immunologic repertoires, ... which, together with the random element of chance, results in the loss or inactivation of many lymphocytes and the receptors they bear.[39]

It is also questionable whether altering immune function would make humans less susceptible to the effects of antigenic variation and antigenic sin. Immunomodulating drugs could influence the immune response to these phenomena but might not control how antigens evolve.

There is yet another factor that can influence the immune response to antigens. T cells may gradually lose their ability to recognize and respond to specific antigens. In T cell exhaustion, there is progressive loss of effector and memory capacity of these cells from persistent antigenic exposure.[40] T cells become less effective in protecting the organism from foreign antigens. This process may affect people differently, depending on the chronicity of the infection and circulation of cancer or infectious cells in the body. Exhaustion in response capacity or depletion in the number of T or B cells may also result from immunosuppressive drugs in organ transplant recipients. It is unclear whether interventions could maintain effector and memory capacity of these cells in the face of antigenic exposure over months or years.

The variability in immune functions among people indicate that the positive or negative effects of interventions in the immune system must be assessed on an individual level and cannot be generalized to the human population as a whole. Their effects in an individual would depend on the four factors outlined above. When genetic factors indicate that an individual may be susceptible to an autoimmune disease, for example, an intervention designed to prevent cross-reactivity between foreign and self-antigens would have to be specific to this phenomenon. If it weakened the natural innate and adaptive response to a pathogenic antigen, then this could make an individual susceptible to an infectious agent before the onset of any autoimmune dysfunction. It might enhance immunity in one respect but weaken it in another. This is one example of how the success or failure of any attempt to optimize immune function to prevent or mitigate immune disorders depends on the complexity of the mechanisms, causes, and modifying factors associated with them.

These considerations suggest a nuanced response to the question raised at the beginning of this section. In principle, the immune system could be enhanced by optimizing interventions that maintained or restored homeostasis in the organism and improved its ability to adapt to and survive in different biological environments. Optimizing immune function would maintain immune fitness in terms of equilibrium and adaptability. This would entail more effective neutralization and elimination of life-threatening antigens, destruction of cancer cells, and tolerance of non-life-threatening antigens. It would also entail preventing or mitigating antigenic mimicry from causing type 1 diabetes, rheumatoid arthritis, lupus, multiple sclerosis, and other autoimmune diseases. It would require balancing immunogenic and tolerogenic responses to foreign and self-antigens so that these responses were neither overactive nor underactive. Interventions designed to change immune functions must not disturb "a balancing act between the need to develop potent effector cells in order to combat foreign pathogens and the need for homeostatic control of the immune system to shut down unwanted autoinflammation, as has been reported in some patients with coronavirus disease and autoimmunity."[41]

Regulation or dysregulation are not intrinsic properties of the immune system but depend on the organism's biological context. They depend on the external environment in which the organism is embedded and how this influences innate and adaptive immune mechanisms within the organism. Interventions designed to improve or enhance immunity must be sensitive to these biological factors and differences among individuals. They must promote balanced activating and inhibiting functions. This in turn can benefit persons by allowing them to have lives free of premature death and disability from hypoactive responses to infections or cancer, or from hyperactive responses in organ-destroying cytokine storms or autoimmune diseases. The description of innate and adaptive immunity in Section 2, and the discussion of how its functions might be optimized in this section, provide an empirical framework for the discussion of the ethical issues they raise in the next five sections.

4 Vaccine Ethics

Vaccines protect people from death and disability caused by infectious agents by activating effector B and T cells and antibodies to neutralize these agents. Immunizations against smallpox, polio, and measles viruses have been among the most effective of these interventions. A new vaccine for malaria could save hundreds of thousands of lives. Recent studies of mRNA vaccines against pancreatic, colon, and breast cancer have had promising results.[42] But this research is at a very early stage. Vaccines induce responses to pathogens or cancer cells that natural or infection-induced acquired humoral and cellular immunity cannot induce on their own. Vaccines can also produce antibodies that prevent noxious substances from entering the brain.

As of January 2023, SARS-CoV-2 had claimed more (likely many more) than 6.7 million lives globally. Different vaccines for this virus have saved an estimated 20 million lives. The mortality rate from severe reactions to COVID-19 vaccination is 8.2 per million population.[43] Most deaths from the virus have been in people older than sixty-five. The benefits of these vaccines clearly outweigh the risks. In addition to preventing severe illness and death, they may also prevent the chronic cognitive and physical impairment from long COVID occurring up to two years or more after infection.[44] "Efficacy" has related but different meanings. It can refer to a vaccine's ability to prevent infection, acute disease, chronic disease, or severe disease leading to death. There are different attitudes and social disagreement about the safety and efficacy of vaccines, however. This disagreement involves ethical questions about how research into developing vaccines is conducted, whether there is an obligation to be vaccinated, or have one's children vaccinated, and how refusal to be inoculated with a vaccine deemed safe and effective may affect one's access to other medical treatments.

The normative landscape of questions about vaccines is vast. I cannot explore all of them in this Element. I will focus on what I take to be the four most ethically controversial issues surrounding immunization: the use of vaccines to treat addiction; the justification of human challenge trials testing vaccines; whether parents are obligated or can refuse to have their children vaccinated against infectious diseases; and whether it is fair to deny a person access to medical treatment because of vaccine refusal.

4.1 Immunological Interventions for Addiction

The general failure of pharmacological interventions to control addiction has generated interest in utilizing immune mechanisms to treat and possibly prevent it. While most of the earlier research involved immunotherapies for cocaine and nicotine addiction, they could be used for opioid addiction as well. This could go some way toward significantly reducing the high number of deaths from overdose of these drugs. As of October 2022, data from the United States Centers for Disease Control and Prevention indicated that more than 100,000 people had died from overdoses.[45]

Vaccines designed to modulate the effects of cocaine and alleviate withdrawal symptoms can generate antibodies that prevent cocaine from crossing the blood-brain barrier. They can also block cocaine receptors in the brain. Vaccines for opioid addiction could have these same blocking effects.[46] The first in-human clinical trial for a vaccine to treat opioid addiction enrolled its first participants in September 2021.[47] The vaccine activates humoral mechanisms to generate antibodies against the oxycodone opioid. These are experimental immune interventions, however, and they will have to overcome many obstacles if they are to become safe and effective in treating or preventing this and other addictive disorders.

Although substance dependence is not an infectious disease, behavior associated with this dependence could put one at risk of contracting such a disease. There has been considerable debate over whether addiction is the result of voluntary but irrational choices by individuals or a neurobiological disease involving dysregulated reward circuitry in the brain.[48] Even if there were professional consensus that addiction involved neural dysregulation, it is not known whether this causes one to make choices resulting in addiction, or whether the dysregulation is the result of choosing to take an addictive substance repeatedly over time. There are genetic and other biological factors that may predispose one to addiction. But addiction is also learned behavior shaped by how one responds to social cues, which include the availability of a substance and the influence of other people's actions. These cannot be explained away by a neurobiological disease model. Indeed, the fact that many commentators point out the need for cognitive behavioral therapy to supplement vaccines as treatments for addiction supports this point.[49] Vaccines alone will not control addictive behavior. Psychological and social interventions are also necessary to control it.

Researchers recruiting subjects for clinical trials testing vaccines for addiction have an obligation to explain the limitations of these trials. In addition to protecting subjects from any adverse effects of the experimental intervention, researchers have an obligation to respect autonomy and ensure that subjects understand the design and purpose of a trial to give informed consent to participate in it. Addiction may compromise a potential research subject's decisional capacity and thus their capacity to consent. This would be determined in the psychological assessment of subjects in the recruitment process.

In their discussion of a vaccine to treat cocaine addiction, Michael Young and coauthors write that "patients associating the efficacy and function of this vaccine ([TA-CD] therapy for addiction-cocaine dependence) with that of other vaccines they have previously received may believe that after they are vaccinated, their cocaine dependency will simply 'dissolve.' Instead, the present formulation of the vaccine does not confer sufficiently high serum concentrations of antibody until 2 weeks into treatment."[50] To ensure that participants gave informed consent to enrollment in a vaccine clinical trial, researchers would have an obligation to disabuse them of any unreasonable expectations about its effects on their addiction. There would also be a need for booster vaccinations over an extended period. Depending on access and patients' motivation to receive boosters in a timely manner, failure to receive them could undermine adherence to a long-term program necessary to control the addiction.

There would be challenges in establishing the efficacy of a vaccine to treat addiction. Research participants in both the active and control groups would have the same addictive disorder. If social cues strongly influence addictive behavior, then observing the direct effects of a vaccine on the reward circuitry in the brain would not be enough to demonstrate that it could control the addiction. Researchers could assess the combined effects of a vaccine and cognitive behavioral therapy against the vaccine alone. But the influence of social cues and socioeconomic burdens in desiring or craving a substance would be difficult to assess in a controlled experimental setting. A vaccine alone would not enable an addict to unlearn learned behavior. These issues would arise in vaccines for opioid addiction as well.

One potential use of a vaccine would be to administer it to criminal offenders whose offenses were associated with an addiction.[51] A vaccine could be incorporated into parole programs to reduce the risk of recidivism and prevent harm to the addict and others who might be adversely affected by their behavior. Again, though, because dysregulation in the brain's reward circuitry is only one aspect of addiction, a vaccine would be just one component of a harm prevention program that would include cognitive behavioral therapy and modification of the person's social network. A vaccine would be offered as a choice rather than forced in a parolee. It could be offered as an intervention intended as one measure to change their behavior and prevent future harm to themselves and others. If it was not forced on but offered to the offender, then it could be a desirable alternative to incarceration. Some might take this to be a coercive offer. An offer is coercive to a person and violates their autonomy when there is no reasonable or desirable alternative, and they believe and feel that they have no choice but to accept it.[52] The person's subjective baseline of well-being is important in assessing such an offer. A person incarcerated for criminal behavior related to addiction could perceive the offer of a vaccine to control addiction and release from incarceration as a desirable alternative to these states. Such an offer could be justified on both rights-based grounds in respecting individual autonomy and consequentialist grounds in preventing harm to oneself and others from criminal acts.[53] But justification would depend on the efficacy of a vaccine for addiction, and research still has not established this.

Vaccines designed to prevent addiction are more scientifically and ethically problematic than those used to treat it. They could be administered in cases where individuals were deemed at risk of addictive behavior based on genetic predisposition, family history, and their social environment. But just because one is genetically predisposed or lives in a socially challenging environment does not imply that the choices they make will inevitably result in addiction. Genetic and epigenetic factors associated with one's socioeconomic context do not necessarily cause one to engage in pathological behavior. It would be difficult for researchers to control for longitudinal factors other than neurobiology in testing whether a vaccine could prevent addiction. Participants in prospective clinical trials testing preventive vaccines would be enrolled based on certain risk factors. But those in the active group receiving the vaccine would be asymptomatic and exposed to any potential adverse effects from it when they might not become addicted. They may be exposed to these effects over time if boosters were included in the trial. Any risk to which these individuals might be exposed would be more difficult to justify than the risks associated with vaccines as treatment for individuals who are addicted. Regarding the TA-CD vaccine, Young and coauthors. comment that "the need for frequent booster vaccinations diminishes the treatment's cost-effectiveness and makes prophylactic use of the present version of the vaccine unlikely."[54] This point can be added to those I have made in questioning the use of preventive vaccines for cocaine, opioid, and indeed all addictions.

Efficacy is not the only consideration is examining how vaccines night be used for addiction. Safety is a more serious consideration. In their 2012 report on early clinical trials of the TA-CD vaccine for cocaine addiction, Young and coauthors stated that "no adverse physiological effects on the brain have been observed."[55] The absence of any direct adverse effects on the brain does not necessarily exclude possible indirect adverse effects. The key issue here is the blood-brain barrier (BBB). One of the functions of the BBB is to prevent infectious agents from crossing it and entering the brain. When they do enter it, blood-borne cytokines like IL-1, IL-6, and TNF-a can cross the BBB and enter cerebrospinal fluid and interstitial fluid spaces of the brain and spinal cord. This is part of the immune system's inflammatory response to pathogens. What is not clear is whether a vaccine that produced antibodies to prevent molecules associated with addictive substances from crossing the BBB would also prevent cytokines from crossing it and thereby prevent a protective immune response to pathogens. Tinkering with the BBB may entail trade-offs between treating addiction and protecting a person from infectious disease. These trade-offs could be avoided by using techniques in delivering vaccines that would block some molecules from entering the brain while allowing others to enter it. This would require a high level of specificity in targeting them. Earlier, I noted that the behavior associated with untreated addiction could put one at risk of contracting an infectious disease. Here, I am suggesting that altering the BBB to treat addiction could also put one at risk. Admittedly, this idea is speculative. But it is an immunological possibility that cannot be ruled out categorically.

Some might argue that the risk-benefit ratio in vaccines for infectious disease is more positive than the ratio in vaccines for addiction. Susceptibility to disability and death from a bacterial or viral infection is worse than living with an addiction. The benefit from avoiding the morbidity and possible mortality from an infection provides a stronger reason to accept the risks associated with a vaccine for a severe infection than a reason to accept the risks associated with a vaccine for addiction. Yet others could argue that the disability, poor quality of life, and shortened lifespan from addiction provide an equally strong reason for accepting the risks associated with vaccines to treat this condition. Crucially, the acceptability of these risks would depend on the efficacy of the vaccine, and "a vaccine will not eliminate the need for other interventions."[56] Unlike preventive interventions for infectious disease, which involve the immune system alone, preventive and therapeutic interventions for addiction involve not only the immune system but also psychological, socioeconomic, and behavioral factors. Variability of these factors, as well as in the neural circuitry among individuals with addiction, can influence how effective vaccines for addiction will be in translating them from research to clinical settings.

4.2 Vaccine Research: Human Challenge Trials

Allowing healthy individuals to participate in medical research testing an experimental drug or procedure may strike some as ethically problematic. It could harm them by causing them to experience adverse physical or psychological events. Although it is rare, in some cases these events can be fatal. Unlike a patient with cancer or a neuropsychiatric disease, healthy individuals experiencing adverse events could be made worse off in absolute terms than those with these diseases because they would be starting from a higher baseline compared with those who were sick. Healthy participants in the control arm of a trial who receive a placebo are not exposed to any risk. Those in the active arm who receive a biochemically active intervention could be at some risk. But if they give informed consent to participate, and if researchers ensure that they are not exposed to more than minimal risk and monitor them throughout the trial, then it can be ethically permissible to allow healthy individuals to participate in this research. It would respect subjects' autonomy and thus be permissible on deontological grounds. By minimizing the risk of a harmful outcome, and generating knowledge about a vaccine, it would also be permissible on consequentialist grounds.

Still, some clinical trials raise ethical concerns about the risks to which healthy participants may be exposed. One example is human challenge trials (HCTs). These involve the intentional exposure of test subjects to a virus or other infectious agent being studied. They enable researchers to gain an understanding of the efficacy of a vaccine against an infectious disease. HCTs have been used to test vaccines to prevent infection from smallpox, polio, and other viruses. Risk in this research can be minimized by isolating participants, close monitoring, and access to therapeutic interventions during and after the trial. They are conducted with low-risk populations. These conditions can make HCTs ethically justifiable. Some have argued that these trials can be ethical despite the risk of adverse events associated with the agent to which they are exposed.[57] But this risk would have to be low, given the potential magnitude of harm to a participant if the risk were realized in one or more severe adverse events.

HCTs do not take as long to complete as field trials. This enables researchers to determine the safety and efficacy of a vaccine in a substantially shorter period than in standard placebo-controlled field trials. It allows more rapid authorization for emergency use in younger and vulnerable populations. Yet one of the limitations of HCTs is that their results are not generalizable to adults. This may not be unique to HCTs because data from many types of medical research are not generalizable from one age group to others. Positive results from challenge trials can allow rapid vaccine rollout that can protect younger people from infectious agents for which there is no vaccine or other effective treatment. They could be followed by completion of field trials in adult participants.[58] The combination of HCTs and field trials could facilitate herd immunity, or an approximation to it, in the general population.

Another concern about HCTs is that, while they provide information on whether a vaccine protects against infection, they do not provide information on whether it prevents severe disease in those who have been infected. This concern is particularly relevant to SARS-CoV-2. Nir Eyal and Tobias Gerhard make five rejoinders to this point:

> First, SARS-CoV-2 vaccine field trials' primary endpoints concerned only mild disease, and they were not powered to confirm impact on severe cases. Second, when HCTs show that a vaccine prevents nasopharyngeal replication, they – importantly – reveal also potential protection of the lungs. Third, a key role for a vaccine is to reduce infections, facilitate herd immunity, and, with other containment measures, end the pandemic. Assessing vaccines in that crucial role is easier with HCTs than in field trials. Fourth, HCTs can complement field trials, with the former assigning vaccine impact on rates of infection and of likely infectiousness . . . and the latter assessing impact on rates of diseases and severe disease. Fifth, the specific division of labor between HCTs and field trials could assign HCTs a merely confirmatory function: when efficacy in reducing infection is confirmed in an HCT, that would suffice for vaccine approval . . .[59]

In sum, HCTs allow rapid approval of vaccines necessary to protect the public from the harm of infectious disease. This protection, and the protection of healthy trial participants' rights not to be exposed to undue risk of adverse events from the vaccine being tested, make these trials justifiable on both consequentialist and deontological grounds.

4.3 Vaccine Mandates and Exemptions

Parents are surrogate decision-makers for their children on medical issues because they lack the cognitive and emotional capacity to make these decisions on their own. It is presumed that parents act in their children's best interests when they make these decisions about medical care and other social goods that are critical for the child's well-being. This is not always the case, however. When parental decisions endanger their child's welfare, or the welfare of others, they may be overridden. There may be limits to parental authority depending on the magnitude of harm that can result from acting or failing to act in certain ways.

The high mortality rate of the bacterial meningococcal disease, and the safety and efficacy of the vaccine for it, provide decisive medical and moral reasons for vaccinating children against this disease. These reasons could not be overridden by any competing reasons for not vaccinating them. Parents are morally obligated to have their children vaccinated to prevent them from being harmed by this disease. The re-emergence of polio, which can cause death and disability from varying degrees of paralysis, also generates a parental obligation to vaccinate children against this virus. Like meningococcal disease, the obligation to have a child vaccinated against polio is based on the magnitude of harm associated with this disease. This motivated authorities in London in August 2022 to offer the polio vaccine to children aged one to nine after the virus was detected in sewage.[60] In New York, children and adults who were never vaccinated against polio have been encouraged to receive the vaccine. What is being offered on a voluntary basis may become mandatory if authorities judge that it is a public health crisis putting the well-being and lives of many people, and especially children, at risk. A public vaccine mandate may override parental refusals of polio vaccine given the severity of the disease.

Some parents object to allowing their children to be vaccinated against the measles virus. Their refusal may be partly influenced by misinformation about the measles vaccine, including adverse effects from it. They may also mistakenly believe that the virus does not pose a serious risk to their children's health and is not highly transmissible to other school-age children. Those refusing to have their children vaccinated may claim that they have a right to make decisions about which medical interventions their children should or should not have. In making these decisions, a parent would be expressing their authority and autonomy in acting in what they believe is their child's best interests.[61] But this authority is limited and can be overridden when parental decisions are contrary to these interests and entail a significant risk of harm to the child. This may also include harm to others with whom their child interacts.

The medical and ethical reasons for vaccination against the measles virus (MV) are compelling. MV is directly responsible for more than 100,000 deaths annually. It is also associated with increased mortality and morbidity for years after infection. The magnitude of harm from severe disease and possible death from MV generates an obligation to vaccinate children to prevent them from being infected. It also justifies overriding parental authority when parents refuse to allow children to be vaccinated against this disease. There is an even more compelling reason for vaccination against MV because it can have adverse effects on the immune system that extend beyond the virus itself.

MV causes acute immune suppression by impairing humoral and cellular memory. As explained in Section 2, the ability of B and T cells to form a memory of an antigen and recognize and respond to it in subsequent encounters is the hallmark of adaptive immunity. Any impairment in this process can compromise the immune system's ability to generate and maintain the requisite level of these cells and antibodies necessary to protect the organism from pathogens. "Epidemiological evidence has associated MV infections with increases in morbidity and mortality for as long as 5 years and suggests that in the pre-vaccine era, MV may have been associated with up to 50% of all childhood deaths from infectious disease, mostly from non-MV infections."[62] These adverse outcomes may be explained in terms of "immune amnesia," which is "a reduction in the diversity of the immune memory repertoire after measles infections."[63] The virus weakens memory B and T cells and epitope-specific antibodies, thereby making those infected by measles susceptible to other infectious agents.

In a study of seventy-seven unvaccinated children before and two months after natural measles virus infection, researchers reported that "measles caused elimination of 11 to 73% of the antibody repertoire across individuals ... The reduction in humoral immune memory after measles infection generates potential vulnerability to future infections, underscoring the need for widespread vaccination."[64] A significant aspect of vulnerability in this population is that children cannot decide to have or refuse a vaccine on their own. Parents make these decisions for them. The need for widespread vaccination, and the magnitude of harm from a highly transmissible virus, generate a moral obligation for parents to have their children vaccinated against MV. If they refuse, then their refusal and parental authority can be overridden by a court-upheld public vaccine mandate that protects the welfare of the child.

The high rate of morbidity and mortality from MV in unvaccinated children makes consequentialist reasons for vaccination outweigh rights-based reasons for parental autonomy in making decisions about vaccination for their children. Vaccinating produces a better outcome than not vaccinating. There is a moral asymmetry in these cases. Assuming that the vaccine is safe and effective, parents can give proxy consent to allow their children to have it. But they may not be permitted to refuse it. Depending on the extent of potential harm from MV infection, there may be limits to parental authority and autonomy in these cases. These limits are supported by J. C. Bester's claim that outbreaks of measles in countries like the United States and United Kingdom are a "moral failure," and that it is "an obvious wrong and an evil to leave children unprotected."[65]

Contractualist moral theory and reasoning offers a way of assessing claims about parental authority regarding vaccination. The transmissibility of a virus makes it a collective rather than individual action problem requiring social cooperation and agreement about how to prevent or limit the extent of harm from it. The idea of agreement is the basis of social contract theory, which has two forms. According to *contractarianism*, rational self-interested agents cooperate with each other because it is mutually advantageous to do so.[66] The aim is to maximize one's own interests in a type of bargain with other like-minded individuals According to *contractualism*, morality is grounded in the equal moral status and mutual respect of persons. The moral status of persons is grounded in their capacity for autonomous rational agency, a view that is traceable to Kant.[67] But contractualism is more than an advanced version of Kantian ethics. It does not involve categorical or hypothetical imperatives about how we should act, and consequences are not excluded from assessing the rightness or wrongness of actions. Instead, the theory states that, in pursuing one's interests, one must be able to justify one's actions to others with their own interests.[68] We justify our actions by appealing to principles that no one could reasonably reject. This is T. M. Scanlon's version of contractualism.[69] A more positive interpretation of this theory is that we justify our actions by appealing to principles that we all could reasonably accept.

Individuals can agree on principles that reflect common social goals and are in everyone's best interests. These include actions on vaccine-preventable diseases. Preventing harm from a virus and thereby preserving people's health and well-being through widespread vaccination are a moral principle and a goal that no one could reasonably reject. Given the importance of individual and parental autonomy, and disagreement about vaccination, this may be a more feasible lower common denominator than the higher common denominator of what all could reasonably accept. Vaccination of adults and children is based on the obvious goods of health and well-being. Widespread vaccination is also consistent with the principle of justice in making safe and effective vaccines for infectious diseases accessible to all. Parental obligation to vaccinate a child against MV would be grounded in the more general obligation to prevent them from being harmed. This includes ensuring that they have an open future free of preventable disease and disability that would lower their quality of life. The claim that failure to vaccinate children who become chronically ill from this virus could limit the child's future liberty supports the case for vaccination.[70]

But not all viruses are equal in their transmissibility and virulence. There are differences in these respects between MV and meningococcal disease, on the one hand, and COVID-19, on the other. Because of differences between adults and children in the risk of contracting an infectious disease, and variability in the severity of disease in those who contract it, parents may retain some degree of autonomy in making decisions about vaccines for their children. Parental authority may be limited in some cases but not others. There may be latitude in these decisions about vaccination, depending on the risk to the child's health from contracting an infectious disease and the relative benefits and risks of an intervention to prevent it.[71]

While children and adolescents with preexisting health conditions are at risk of serious disease and death from the COVID-19 virus, otherwise healthy children and adolescents who contract it are at lower risk of severe disease than adults. This risk is lower than it is from meningococcal disease, measles, and other infectious diseases. The risk of chronic cognitive, emotional, and physical symptoms from long COVID also appears to be lower in children than it is for younger and older adults. This may vary across jurisdictions. To cite one example, as of September 14, 2022, it was estimated that 80 percent of children in British Columbia had had COVID-19, but most of them had had mild symptoms.[72] There is also lack of clarity on the risk of transmissibility of this virus in elementary and middle schools. These considerations raise questions about relative risks and benefits of a vaccine and may provide reasons against mandatory vaccination of children. For some parents, the generally mild symptoms associated with the virus and the risk of vaccine-induced sequelae, albeit low, may lead them to conclude that the vaccine would not confer substantial benefit on their child, and that any benefit would not outweigh this risk. Rational skepticism that the vaccine would confer substantial benefit may justify giving parents some discretion in whether or not to have their children vaccinated.[73] The degree to which parents have this discretion depends on the transmissibility and severity of the infectious disease among children.

Nevertheless, health authorities may argue that vaccinating children against this virus is clearly in their best interests. They could cite a study showing that the mRNA-1273 vaccine is safe in children from six months to five years of age and that it induces an immune response similar to that in young adults.[74] They could argue that vaccinating children aged five to eleven is also in the interests of adults to whom children might transmit the virus. Those with preexisting medical conditions could be susceptible to severe disease. Healthy adults could be susceptible to long COVID. Widespread vaccination of all age groups, including children, would be the default position if the virus were considered a public health crisis requiring collective action. Vaccination could be mandated as necessary to maintain public health.

Many countries have mandated vaccination for those aged twelve to fifteen, and even younger. California did the same in 2022, with the state acting as *parens patriae*. The claim that vaccination protects public health could override parental authority if parents refused to allow their children to be vaccinated. But this default position would depend on the transmissibility of the disease and the risk of disease, disability, and death associated with the virus. It would also depend on the safety and efficacy of the vaccine. These criteria could be used to draw boundaries on permissible parental decisions about vaccinating children.[75]

In the case of COVID-19 and certain other infectious diseases, there may be uncertainty about the relative benefits and risks of vaccines and thus uncertainty about where exactly these boundaries should be drawn. It can be difficult to demarcate zones of parental authority. In the United States alone, approximately

17 percent of the more than sixty million cases of SARS-CoV-2 have been among children. But children account for less than 3 percent of all hospitalizations. By 2022, approximately 750 children had died from the virus in the USA, or 0.1 percent of all deaths.[76] But it has had a significant adverse impact on their education, mental health, and other aspects of their lives. The Pfizer vaccine was FDA-approved for minors aged twelve and older. It is also available to children between five and eleven under an emergency use authorization.

Whether parents are permitted to make these decision for adolescents (twelve years and older) is a more complex issue. Unlike children, some adolescents may have the cognitive and emotional capacity to know what is in their best interests and make decisions about vaccines and other medical interventions that are consistent with their interests. It is complex because decisional capacity comes in degrees, and whether an adolescent has this capacity may not always be clear. "Mature minors" may have enough capacity to understand the benefits and risks of vaccines and make an informed decision to have or refuse vaccination. Others may not have enough of this capacity, and parents would be their substitute decision-makers.

The risk of myocarditis associated with the messenger RNA (mRNA) vaccine for SARS-CoV-2 predominantly affects adolescent males and young adults (fourteen to thirty years of age). This may influence a parent's decision about whether their child should be vaccinated.[77] One could argue for asymmetry in these cases, allowing adolescents to consent to vaccination independently of their parents, but not allowing them to refuse vaccination without parental consent. This argument would be based on the potential harm from refusing vaccination. But if an adolescent is mature enough to know what is in their best interests, then they alone should make this decision. If the adolescent lacks the requisite maturity, and the parent refuses to consent for them, then the public health risk imposed by COVID-19 or similar virus could justify mandatory vaccination for middle and high school entry.[78] Adolescents who are home-schooled would be exempt because they could not transmit the virus to other students. A mandate would be based on the potential adverse health effects of the virus, its transmissibility in school settings, and the relative safety and efficacy of the vaccine in preventing harm from the virus.

Vaccine mandates for adults have been more controversial because of claims that it unjustifiably restricts their liberty. Some argue that the harm from this restriction is worse than the harm from contracting the virus. Yet for workers who are exposed to large numbers of people, such as those in the service industry, teachers in elementary and secondary schools and universities, and especially health care workers exposed to patients, a vaccine mandate to prevent contracting and transmitting a virus causing relatively high rates of morbidity and mortality could not be reasonably rejected.

The 1905 United States Supreme Court case of *Jacobson v. Massachusetts* serves as a legal precedent supporting the argument for vaccine mandates in a public health crisis.[79] The Court upheld the authority of states to enforce compulsory vaccination to eradicate smallpox. They argued that individual liberty is not absolute and may be subject to the police power of the state when there is a clear health emergency. The high degree of transmissibility, disease, and death from smallpox justified limiting individual liberty to refuse vaccination. This is supported by John Stuart Mill's principle of liberty. Mill says that "over himself, over his own body and mind, the individual is sovereign."[80] Yet he also says that "the only purpose for which power can be rightfully exercised over any member of a civilized community, against his will, is to prevent harm to others."[81] When there is a public health crisis, and an individual's behavior can harm others, the first formulation of Mill's liberty principle can be overridden by the second. There may be exemptions from these mandates, though they would depend on the extent of an individual's exposure to others, the risk of transmission, and the virulence of the virus. Exemptions on religious grounds are difficult to justify because one's religious beliefs are not directly related to how one's immune system is affected by a virus or responds to a vaccine.

Could an adverse response to a vaccine at an earlier time justify an exemption from being mandated to receive a different vaccine at a later time? In *Jacobson v. Massachusetts*, Cambridge pastor Henning Jacobson refused to be vaccinated against smallpox. He claimed that he and his son had an adverse reaction to and had suffered from an earlier vaccination while living in Sweden. Jacobson argued that involuntary vaccination was a violation of the Fourteenth Amendment, which says that no state can deprive its citizens of life, liberty or property without due process of law. But the Court ruled 7–2 that mandatory vaccination did not violate the Amendment in this case. They reasoned that "in every well-ordered society charged with the duty of conserving the safety of its members, the rights of the individual in respect of his liberty may at times, under the pressure of great dangers, be subjected to such restraint, to be enforced by reasonable regulation, as the safety of the general public may demand."[82] By citing smallpox as a great danger, the Court implicitly endorsed Mill's limiting condition on individual liberty.

Still, an individual who had an earlier adverse reaction to a vaccine may reasonably claim that they should not be vaccinated again. This claim would be based not only on the potential physical harm from adverse effects of the vaccine but also on the psychological harm from being anxious about experiencing these effects again. SARS-CoV-2 may not present the same threat to public health as smallpox did in 1905. But it is a clear threat, nonetheless. Individuals who could present evidence of natural immunity from the virus could be exempt from vaccination.[83] In other cases, whether a claim for exemption against a vaccine for SARS-CoV-2 or other viruses could be morally and legally permissible would depend not only on the individual's experience with previous vaccines but also the number of people who could be exposed to and infected by the unvaccinated individual. If they were socially and physically isolated and competent to make medical decisions, then even immunocompromised individuals at high risk of becoming severely ill and dying from the virus could refuse it. The individual would have a right to refuse it as an expression of their autonomy, regardless of the consequences for them. If they were not exposed to others, then they could refuse to be vaccinated. One could appeal to the first formulation of Mill's principle of liberty to support this decision. The second formulation would not apply in such a case.

It is important to distinguish between moderate and severe adverse effects. Only moderately severe to severe adverse effects on cardiorespiratory, neurological, and other systems from a previous vaccination would provide medical grounds for an exemption from subsequent vaccinations. Moderate effects may not provide these grounds. Indeed, one study concluded that symptoms such as fever, chills, and muscle pain from mRNA vaccines against SARS-CoV-2 were associated with a stronger antibody response to the virus.[84] This supports the general claim that the overall benefit of a vaccine medically and morally outweighs any harm that might result from it.

4.4 Vaccination and Access to Medical Care

Doctors have a fiduciary responsibility to their patients and thus a duty to provide care to meet patients' medical needs. This type of responsibility implies an unequal relationship between the physician and the patient, where the first has more control in decision-making than the second. The duty of care is not contingent on how these needs develop but is generated by the needs themselves. Correlations between certain lifestyle choices and certain diseases are not sufficient to establish a causal connection between them. Even a causal connection between them would not weaken the physician's duty of care and would not justify treating patients unequally in providing care for them. Fairness consists in meeting needs in proportion to their strength.[85] When different patients have the same medical need, and there is equal strength in their claim to have this need met, it would be unfair to give lower priority to some patients rather than give all patients equal access to care.

There may be cases, however, in which it may be fair to give lower priority in access to care to some patients when a specific action or omission results in medical need and a claim to receive care. Fiduciary responsibility does not imply that a patient has no control over the process that generates the need. An example would be vaccination status as a criterion for allocating beds in intensive care unit (ICU) triage. Unvaccinated patients who develop end-stage organ failure and need an organ transplant may also justifiably be given lower priority on the transplant waiting list if being unvaccinated entails a high probability of organ failure after transplantation. Although the reasons for lower priority in these two types of cases are different, they are based on the consequentialist principle that the right action or policy in a given situation is one that brings about a better outcome than any alterative action or policy in terms of its effects on people's health and well-being. Consequentialism has more moral weight than rights-based deontological theories when a medical resource is scarce and cannot be provided to all in need. It should be allocated to maximize good in ensuring survival and restoring health when the needs of all cannot be met. But deontological considerations are relevant here as well.

David Shaw argues that vaccination status could be a criterion in assessing claims about equality and priority in ICU admission. There are unique features of COVID-19 vaccination that make it disanalogous to the relation between smoking and lung cancer, or alcoholism and end-stage liver disease, in these respects. He gives three reasons for this position:

> First, there is equality in access to care at the point of vaccination; the unvaccinated refuse the offer of preventive care when they decline vaccination, weakening their claim to ongoing care if they become ill ... Second, the decision of one person to refuse vaccination substantially increases the risk that they will become seriously ill and need ICU care ... which increases the pressure on intensive care bed provision, as well as increasing the risk that he or she will infect others who in turn might end up needing ICU care. Third, justice cuts both ways, and giving unvaccinated patients equal priority may itself be unjust when other patients have reduced their risk of ending up in the ICU by getting vaccinated.[86]

In allocating a scarce medical resource like ICU care, it is generally fair to give greater weight to those with greater needs and equal weight to those with the same need. But sometimes it may not be fair to give equal weight to the claims of those with equal medical need. Whether there is an obligation to meet a patient's claim to receive care for a medical need may be influenced by how the need arose. Specifically, whether there is an obligation to meet a person's claim of need for intensive care due to a severe viral infection may depend on whether a voluntary choice to refuse vaccination caused them to need this care.

A consequentialist interpretation says that a just distribution of a scarce resource like intensive care is one that maximizes benefit and minimizes harm. This would mean giving higher priority for ICU admission to admitting patients who are more likely to survive and lower priority to those less likely to survive.[87] A patient vaccinated to prevent infection from a highly virulent virus would be more likely to survive than an unvaccinated one.

A deontological interpretation of justice could include consideration of how the need for intensive care arose. Suppose that one patient refuses vaccination and becomes severely ill with COVID-19. A second patient has been vaccinated and develops a different but equally severe illness beyond their control. Priority in access to critical care could be given to the second patient over the first. It could be unfair to give equal weight to the claims of the unvaccinated and vaccinated to receive intensive care if the first but not the second acted to prevent severe disease requiring intensive care.

Nonconsequentialism may offer a more satisfactory defense of this judgment. According to this theory, the justification of an action is not solely determined by the goodness or badness of its consequences. Outcomes matter morally. But there is no absolute obligation to bring them about, and concern about outcomes does not always override the interests and rights of individuals. "Nonconsequentialism is now typically thought to include the prerogative not to maximize the good and constraints on producing the good."[88] Consistent with this view, one could argue that lower priority to the unvaccinated for ICU care could be justified because of the direct connection between individual voluntary choice and the outcome of that choice for them. The reasoning behind this judgment is not based on an impersonal calculus about outcomes but on voluntary choice and taking responsibility for its consequences. The choice not to be vaccinated could weaken a person's claim to care if they became infected and could give them lower priority for ICU admission. This is an example of how it may be fair in some instances to treat people and their claims unequally despite having the same need. Still, the strength of this argument depends on the strength of physicians' fiduciary responsibility to care for patients in need, regardless of how that need arose.

There is a factor of luck that can weaken arguments for lower priority for critical care to the unvaccinated.[89] Some unvaccinated people do not become infected and do not need this care. But knowing the risk of infection in refusing vaccination can be enough to make them at least partly responsible for it and thereby weaken their claim to care, even if this leaves something to chance. Intensivists who uphold fiduciary responsibility to patients would not accept this argument. This responsibility is not conditional on patient choices and applies to all types of acute medical need. They would insist that all patients with this need, including the unvaccinated who developed severe SARS-CoV-2, should have equal access to the ICU. Their decision not to be vaccinated should not give them lower priority than others who were vaccinated but had other life-threatening conditions. The only permissible inequality would be based on consequentialist reasoning in giving lower priority in access to this scarce resource to those less likely to survive.[90] Yet others would insist that voluntary choices have morally significant consequences and that they could affect claims to critical care for conditions that are among these consequences. Physicians' duty to provide appropriate care for their patients is not the only morally significant issue here. Competent patients have the right to refuse medical interventions such as vaccinations. Exercising this right entails taking responsibility for what results from it, including severe illness. The patient's personal responsibility may be just as morally significant as the physician's fiduciary responsibility.

Would these same considerations apply to organ transplantation? Transplant *recipients* are at greater risk of contracting and becoming severely ill from SARS-CoV-2 and other infectious diseases than the general population. Immunosuppressive drugs that prevent organ rejection cause T cell depletion that can make them immunocompromised. Transplant recipients do not respond as well to vaccines as healthy individuals. But "the likelihood of at least partial response, higher risk of severe disease, and risk of spreading SARS-CoV-2 variants strongly lean in favor of vaccination."[91] There are questions about how many doses transplant recipients should receive, and when to administer them. But fundamentally there is a strong reason for vaccination.

The medical and ethical issues surrounding vaccination may be different for transplant *candidates*. Should people in end-stage organ failure and in need of an organ transplant have equal access to and have an equal claim to a transplant as others if they refuse vaccination? Patients with end-stage organ failure typically have poor vaccine responses.[92] Their immune systems may already be compromised from disease before transplantation. Drugs like tacrolimus or sirolimus that suppress a natural immune response to HLA to prevent graft rejection would compromise them further. Those waiting for an organ transplant who refuse vaccination would be at higher risk of contracting an infection that could increase the risk of death. The American Society of Transplantation, the International Society of Heart and Lung Transplantation, and the American Society of Transplant Surgeons "all generally recommend vaccinating transplant recipients because of their higher risk of severe illness and death from COVID-19."[93] Vaccine-hesitant transplant candidates and recipients "should be provided with sufficient information about vaccine safety and COVID-19 risk without force or judgment, and they should be allowed to make their own decision."[94] This would include information about the risk of permanent lung damage from the virus from infection and the need for a lung transplant to remain alive.

An informed voluntary decision about vaccination can either prevent or result in harm to the person who makes it. If transplant candidates refuse to be vaccinated, then they could become severely ill and die from infection following a transplant. Because organs are scarce, and because being unvaccinated puts a transplant recipient at higher risk of a poor transplant outcome, in principle those who voluntarily refuse vaccination and know the risk of refusing it could be given lower priority on the transplant waiting list. Consequentialist reasons could be used to fairly discriminate between vaccinated and unvaccinated patients. Rights-based reasons could also be used to support this position because the right to make decisions about which medical interventions to have or refuse entails taking responsibility for the consequences of these decisions. As in the case of access to the ICU, one could argue for lower priority in access to an organ transplant based on a specific voluntary decision about a safe and effective intervention that could prevent a poor outcome in allocating a scarce resource. Access to care in these cases may depend on how one's decision to refuse a preventive intervention influences the outcome of that care.

In a November 2022 ruling, The Alberta (Canada) Court of Appeal used similar reasoning to uphold the requirement that eligible transplant recipients be vaccinated against COVID-19. Alberta Health Services refused to put a patient with ideopathic pulmonary fibrosis on the waiting list for a double-lung transplant because she refused to be vaccinated. She refused despite the significant risk the virus entails for immunocompromised transplant recipients. The patient filed a legal challenge against the health authority, claiming that her charter rights to life, conscience, liberty, and security of her person were violated. Agreeing with an earlier legal judgment, the Court ruled that her rights were not violated, and that vaccination against COVID-19 was established medical treatment for people needing and seeking an organ transplant. A patient can refuse a vaccine. But the consequences of this refusal, including death from failure of the transplanted organ to function, would be caused by the patient rather than the health care providers.[95] These same issues will arise in future epidemics and pandemics among immunocompromised and unvaccinated patients needing acute medical care.

5 Immuno-Oncology

Cancer can be defined as "a breakdown of multicellular cooperation that manifests in uncontrolled proliferation."[96] In healthy individuals, macrophages and the cytokine TNF-a control abnormal cell growth that otherwise would result in cancer. But cancer cells can mutate and adapt to these mechanisms and evade immune surveillance. Chemotherapy destroys cancer cells but can also destroy healthy cells, tissues, and organs. Cancer cells can evade the effects of these drugs as well. Immuno-oncology can control proliferation of these cells into tumors and metastases by modifying T lymphocytes to target and eradicate them from the body. The basic idea is to manipulate the immune system to induce an antitumor response. Cancer vaccines, monoclonal antibodies (MAs), immune checkpoint inhibitors (ICIs), and chimeric antigen receptor T cell (CAR T-cell) therapy use genetically engineered T cells to achieve this goal. Interferon gamma is a cytokine that, in addition to mediating inflammation, may be modified as another form of immune therapy for cancer.

I mentioned experimental cancer vaccines in Section 4. I discuss the use of monoclonal and polyclonal antibodies against pathogens in Section 7. Here I focus on empirical and moral aspects of MAs, ICIs, and CAR T in immuno-oncology. These interventions have been effective in controlling different cancers that have not responded or have ceased to respond to chemotherapy or radiation. But immunotherapies may induce certain toxicities and other adverse effects that must be factored into their medical and moral benefit-risk calculus.

Trastuzumab is a recombinant monoclonal antibody that is an FDA-approved treatment for Herceptin 2-positive breast cancer. This is an engineered protein designed to target specific sections of cancer cells. While this therapy has been very effective on the whole, not all people with this type of breast cancer respond to it. When it is effective, there are risks if it is combined with chemotherapy. These include fever and, more seriously, high circulating levels of pro-inflammatory cytokines within the body. As noted, these can damage healthy cells, tissues, and organs. Another concern is that monoclonal antibodies could make patients susceptible to viral infections. Variants of the SARS-CoV-2 virus, or other pathogens, could escape weak immune responses from patients who are immunocompromised from cancer. "In the absence of effective immune responses, selective pressures such as those from monoclonal antibody treatment may lead to the emergence of immunologically important mutations."[97] In general, though, when monoclonal antibodies destroy cells and tumor development in breast and other cancers, the benefits outweigh the risks. This depends on how the patient experiences cancer remission and, if there are adverse effects, how they weigh life extension with the therapy against their quality of life. In some cases, adverse effects may be severe enough to discontinue monoclonal antibody therapy. Patients must then seek therapeutic alternatives in discussion with their oncologists, families, and other forms of social support.

ICIs treat cancers using monoclonal antibodies that target programmed cell death and programmed cell death ligand.[98] Immune checkpoints are proteins that normally become activated when proteins on the surface of T cells (such as PD-1) recognize and bind to proteins on other cells, including tumor cells (such as PD-L1). When these two types of proteins bind together, they can deactivate or cause T cells to dysfunction, thereby allowing tumor growth. ICIs block this binding and allow T cells to kill cancer cells. Immune checkpoint inhibitors have been effectively used as therapy for breast and lung cancers, lymphoma, melanoma, and other cancers. But not all patients respond favorably to them. In melanoma, for example, "approximately half these patients will not have a durable benefit."[99] They can also result in a unique set of immune-related adverse events.[100] These are different from standard chemotherapy toxicities and can occur when ICIs are used separately or combined with chemotherapy.

ICIs may involve toxicities associated with hyperinflammatory or other mechanisms that can damage organ systems.[101] They can induce cytokine release syndrome or activate autoantibodies in a process resulting in auto-immune disease. In one case of an ICI used to treat a patient with advanced lung cancer, the patient developed autoimmune thyroiditis.[102] Manipulating the immune system to eliminate tumor cells may unintentionally cause immune dysregulation and harmful effects that can offset the benefits in some patients receiving the intervention. Accordingly, ICIs require the same monitoring of patients and constant assessment of their effects as radiation and chemotherapy. While there are differences in their biological mechanisms, there is no morally significant difference between adverse events from ICIs and adverse events from chemotherapy. What matters is how these events affect a patient's func-tional capacities, whether they cause pain and suffering, or whether they avoid these negative experiences and restore these capacities. ICIs may destroy cancer cells and tumors more effectively and cause fewer adverse events than chemo-therapy. Nevertheless, the overall benefit will depend on whether they can extend a patient's life and improve their quality of life.

In CAR T-cell therapy, T cells are genetically modified to target and destroy cancer cells expressing tumor markers. "Autologous T cells can be genetic-ally engineered in vitro to become tumor reactive by the introduction of genes that encode receptors specific for tumor antigens (either T cell receptors [TCRs] or chimeric antigen receptors [CARs])." Both forms of T cell engin-eering could overcome T cell exhaustion, where the cells are reduced to a "hyporesponsive state"[103] from persistent encounters with tumor antigens. They would restore the ability of T cells to "produce the effector cytokines (TNF-a, interferon-gamma, and interleukin-2) and cytotoxic molecules (granzymes and perforin) that are necessary for effective attack and elimination of tumor cells."[104] A study published in early 2022 showed that two patients with lymphocytic leukemia who received this type of immunotherapy had a sustained remission and detectable CAR-T cells ten years after being infused with them.[105]

In addition to leukemia, genetically modified autologous T cells have been used to eliminate tumors in some patients with lymphoma, multiple myeloma, and melanoma. Macrophages are the main regulators of T cell activation. They can be recruited to activate T cells and in turn destroy cancer cells driving tumor development and progression. But macrophages can either activate or inhibit T cells based on their phenotype.[106] An intervention intended to kill cancer cells by increasing activating and decreasing inhibitory T cell mechanisms would have to target a specific macrophage phenotype. Macrophages can also induce cytokine secretion and thus inflammation. The targeting would have to be specific here as well to avoid chronic hyperinflammation that could destroy not only cancer cells but also healthy cells. TNF-based "designer cytokines" could target tumor vasculature and induce cancer remission.[107] "Designer" suggests the requisite level of specificity to destroy tumors and avoid collateral damage. It would require targeting the right inflammatory mediators and maintaining a balance of pro-inflammatory and anti-inflammatory mechanisms. This outcome would depend on how natural and engineered cytokines interacted with macrophages and myeloid cells, which can promote or slow tumor progression.

Further research will determine whether T cells can be modified with a level of specificity to both destroy cancer cells and leave healthy cells intact. This would benefit and avoid harmful effects in patients undergoing TCR or CAR T-cell therapy. One recent phase 3 trial comparing tumor-infiltrating lymphocyte (TIL) therapy with the monoclonal antibody ipilimumab showed that patients with advanced melanoma receiving TIL had longer progression-free survival.[108] More studies are needed to establish whether this intervention is superior to ICIs in controlling cancer.

Immunotherapy may be considered a treatment of last resort for many cancer patients who have failed to respond to other treatments. Even it they consider it in this way, this does not imply that patients are not capable of considering the risk of adverse effects and lack the cognitive capacity to consent to receive it in a clinical setting or a randomized controlled clinical trial. Some patients may have a therapeutic misconception in agreeing to participate in a trial designed to determine the safety and efficacy of a drug if a patient believes that they will directly benefit from it.[109] But this does not mean that they lack the capacity to consent to participate in the trial. Their desire and hope for remission can be consistent with their capacity to rationally process information about the treatment and the trial.

Some patients may not give much thought to the risk of toxicity to organs or autoimmune disease from immunotherapy. But their decision to receive it can be voluntary and autonomous. Others who give more thought to potential sequelae may accept this risk and rationally decide to receive immunotherapy to thwart an immediate threat and give them a last chance of extending their lives. Oncologists could allay a patient's fear and anxiety by not presenting immunotherapy as a treatment of last resort but as a treatment option when other options have not been effective, or when the patient is not a candidate for them. They could explain that immunotherapy is not a first-line treatment because the long-term effects of manipulating the immune system to treat cancer are not fully known. By presenting immunotherapy as another treatment option rather than the last possible treatment, they would not be deceiving the patient. They would be discharging their duties of beneficence and nonmaleficence to them.[110]

Some researchers have claimed that cancer patients might benefit more if immunotherapy were initiated at an earlier stage of disease.[111] It could be used instead of chemotherapy to prevent the disease from becoming refractory to treatment. Randomized controlled clinical trials conducted at an earlier stage of disease that determined the safety and efficacy of ICIs, TCR, and CAR T-cell therapy could lead to accelerated approval that could achieve this therapeutic goal. Julia Beaver and Richard Pazdur write: "Although single-arm trials enrolling patients with an unmet medical need may provide a new therapy for patients with refractory disease, this approach may delay trials in patients with earlier-stage, less refractory disease, who might benefit more."[112] Randomized trials enrolling patients with less advanced cancer "provide the opportunity to characterize safety more fully and to examine other efficacy end points, including progression-free survival and overall survival."[113]

Compared with double-arm clinical trials, single-arm trials have modest effect sizes and are more susceptible to bias.[114] Without a control group, the second type of trial is less scientifically robust than the first. This can influence the interpretation of the data and the final assessment of the trial. But they can expedite drug approval, which can take longer in randomized controlled trials. Single-arm active trials without a control group might preclude a therapeutic misconception about their purpose. All patients in the trial would receive an active intervention. If the trials enrolled patients with early-stage cancer, then presumably they would not be motivated by desperation to participate in a trial because it would not be the only or the last treatment option. Some patients in single-arm and double-arm randomized controlled trials may still not fully consider the risks of the intervention. Yet if they were fully informed by

researchers of the design, purpose, and known and unknown risks of participating in the trial, then they could voluntarily consent to participate in it.

There may be negative psychological implications of using immunotherapy
as first-line treatment, especially if cancer patients fail to respond to it, or
respond for only a limited period. The implications could be especially significant if a patient believes that immunotherapy is more likely to destroy cancer
cells and tumors and induce remission than any alternative therapy. It could be
psychologically worse for a patient to go from a treatment considered medically
advanced to one considered medically standard if they failed to respond to the
first treatment and had the second as the only option. It could influence their
attitudes and emotions about their chances of survival, which they may believe
are lower with chemotherapy than they were with immunotherapy. Depending
on their knowledge of immunotherapy, a cancer patient may be more hopeful
about extending their life if their treatment regimen first included chemotherapy
and then immunotherapy, rather than the other way around. To be sure, if
immunotherapy initiated at an early stage of cancer eliminated tumor cells
and induced long-term remission, then the negative psychological states associated with a transition from immunotherapy to radiation and/or chemotherapy
would not arise. There would be both a positive physiological response from the
body and a positive psychological response from the patient. Still, immunotherapy may not always be the most effective treatment for cancer patients at
different stages of their disease.

The speed with which immune checkpoint inhibitors and chimeric antigen
receptor T-cell therapy have been FDA-approved leaves questions about their
long-term effects in cancer patients. There is a need for greater coordination in
conducting clinical trials with these agents and approving them for treatment.
While their efficacy has been demonstrated in certain cancers, there is still an
incomplete understanding of their safety, especially their toxicity. Oncologists
who treat patients or enroll them as research subjects in clinical trials, and
patients themselves, must factor this uncertainty into their decisions to administer or receive immunotherapy

6 Neuroimmunology

There is bidirectional communication between central and peripheral nervous
systems (CNS and PNS) and the immune system. This is necessary both to
maintain homeostasis in the organism and to protect it from pathogenic threats
to the brain. Immune cells interact with neurons to change their properties.[115]
Some of these changes are part of a coordinated defense against these threats.
Others involve dysregulated immune functions in the body and brain that can

make us susceptible to neurodevelopmental and neurodegenerative disorders. In this section, I examine interventions that might prevent or mitigate the effects of certain neuropathologies. Given the interactions between the nervous and immune systems, these interventions must target both systems to be effective.

Whether the brain is healthy or diseased depends to a great extent on the activity of microglia and cytokines. Microglia are specialized macrophage immune cells that constitute 5–10 percent of all brain cells. Their "main functions are to maintain CNS homeostasis and to provide rapid responses to damage or infection."[116] They clear cellular waste from the brain and have a key role in neurogenesis and neurodevelopment in childhood and adolescence. The BBB is critical in maintaining homeostasis by preventing pathogens from infiltrating the brain. Without infiltration, there would not be any cells or molecules to induce a microglial response. "The BBB prevents 98% of antibodies and small molecules from entering the brain parenchyma."[117] But this is enough to allow some pathogens to enter the brain. Microglia then become activated to destroy them.

Macrophages and T cells can also cross the BBB under certain conditions. While these cells ordinarily protect the organism from infectious agents, in some instances they can disrupt neuromodulating mechanisms and have damaging effects if they enter the brain. This suggests that certain immune cells can protect the brain, and that others may damage it. Even microglia can cause brain damage if they become hyperactive and trigger high levels of inflammation in response to an infectious agent. While the response of microglia to pathogens or other immune cells entering the brain is normally neuroprotective, too strong a response can result in neuropathology. One neuroimaging study using positron-emission tomography (PET) has shown elevated microglial activity and neuroinflammation in people at very high risk of psychosis and schizophrenia.[118] Also, microglial reactions to certain viruses may result in neuronal cell death.[119] Intravenous infusion of immunoglobins can mitigate this response and prevent neuronal damage. But this may not stop pathogenesis in all cases. More significantly, intravenous immunoglobin to modulate microglial function may cause hematologic toxicities in the brain.[120]

Microglia also mediate synaptic pruning, which is a natural process of normal brain development that occurs in childhood and adolescence. Approximately 40 percent of the total number of synapses in the brain are eliminated during this period. Genetic and epigenetic factors can cause these processes to become dysregulated in some brains. Hyperactivated microglia may prune too many synapses. This excess pruning is one hypothesis for the pathogenesis of neurodevelopmental disorders such as schizophrenia and major depression.[121]

Cytokines are present in the brain as well as the body. Microglia and other CNS cells such as neurons and astrocytes can produce cytokines. In addition to mediating inflammation, cytokines have a critical role in maintaining neuroplasticity. It is not the inflammatory action per se of cytokines that causes neuronal dysregulation. On the contrary, this is an essential property of its protective and neurogenerative functions. Rather, "excess or prolonged inflammatory cytokine activity perturbs multiple neuronal functions."[122] Although pro-inflammatory cytokines in the body are relatively large molecules, they can influence brain function by crossing "leaky" sections of the BBB.[123] Related to its association with neurodegenerative disease, neuroinflammation can impair neurotransmitter signaling and disrupt the "synthesis, reuptake, and release of neurotransmitters."[124] Major depressive disorder (MDD) is associated with this disruption due to high levels of cytokine activation and inflammation in the brain.[125] Dysregulated cytokine alterations have also been linked to schizophrenia. A subset of people with this disease has neuroimflammation in regions such as the dorsolateral prefrontal cortex.[126]

The neuroinflammation resulting from these alterations has been implicated in chronic post-viral syndromes like myalgic encephalomyelitis/chronic fatigue syndrome (ME/CFS) and long COVID.[127] Viral infections can activate neuroinflammatory microglia, cytokines, and chemokines that can inhibit neurogenesis in cortical and subcortical brain regions manifesting in chronic cognitive impairment, fatigue, and other symptoms.[128] It is estimated that one in five people infected with SARS-CoV-2 suffer from long COVID.[129]

It is possible that certain interventions in the brain could modulate microglial activity and synaptic pruning and thus prevent or mitigate the effects of neuroinflammation and excess pruning implicated in neurodevelopmental disorders. It is also possible that interventions could modulate microglia and cytokine activity in the brain to prevent excess inflammation associated with autoimmune diseases such as multiple sclerosis and neurodegenerative disorders. In conditions where neuropathology is already present, neuromodulating agents might mitigate the effects of dysregulation and ameliorate symptoms in affected people. More speculatively, it may be possible for certain agents to stop or reverse these pathologies by inducing neuroprotective and neurogenerative mechanisms. The therapeutic implications of these interventions would be significant, given the hundreds of millions of people who suffer from these disorders. Collectively, they cause considerable harm to affected people by causing a high degree of morbidity and, in many cases, premature mortality. For example, "the morbidity and mortality associated with major depression renders it the number one cause of disability world-wide and exerts an extraordinary burden on society in terms of lost productivity."[130] The neuropsychiatric sequelae of chronic post-viral autoimmune and other syndromes add to this burden.

To date, however, no anti-inflammatory agents have been able to prevent or reverse the pathogenesis of these disorders. In schizophrenia, "small therapeutic trials of anti-inflammatory agents targeting immune function have been consistently negative."[131] To avoid psychological harm from unmet therapeutic expectations, patients' and caregivers' attitudes must align with the state of the research. Nevertheless, novel neuromodulating agents may have the potential to control the pathophysiology and symptoms of some neuropsychiatric disorders.

As these agents are developed and tested, they must overcome one critical obstacle. The ability of any intervention to modulate brain activity depends on its ability to cross the BBB. Yet this barrier is designed to prevent most small molecules from entering the brain. This could prevent the type of agents I have mentioned from having any preventive or therapeutic effect. Techniques such as magnetic resonance-guided focused ultrasound may open the BBB to allow agents to modulate microglia activity, synaptic pruning, and neuroinflammatory mechanisms. These could prevent or limit the extent of neuronal dysfunction associated with neuropsychiatric disorders. As noted in the discussion of vaccines for addiction, though, opening the BBB to allow certain molecules to enter the brain for a therapeutic purpose might also allow other molecules to enter it. This may cause or exacerbate the dysfunction and damage that opening the barrier was intended to prevent, reduce, or reverse. Delivering neuroprotective or neurogenerative agents through the BBB and preventing molecules that would cause neural dysfunction would require a high degree of spatial and temporal specificity in opening and closing it. This would determine whether the intervention was beneficial or harmful to the patient. Noninvasive light irradiation to modulate microglia might be a safer but not necessarily more effective technique.

Let us assume that neuroprotective agents could be developed to target specific neuroimmune dysfunction and preserve normal neuronal function. PET, diffusion tensor imaging (DTI), and functional magnetic resonance imaging (fMRI) can detect elevated levels of microglial and cytokine activity associated with this dysfunction. Clinical trials have been conducted to investigate how interfering with and modulating high levels of microglia activity could ameliorate positive (hallucinations and delusions) and negative (cognitive impairment, flat affect, social withdrawal, avolition) symptoms of schizophrenia and possibly prevent them.[132] Given the presence of this biomarker, one early intervention could be the antibiotic minocycline to regulate the rate of synaptic pruning.[133] In a different intervention, the muscarinic acetylcholine receptor agonist xanomeline has improved subjects' cognition in phase 2 trials in Alzheimer's disease and schizophrenia.[134] Other drugs crossing the BBB could modulate chronic inflammatory cytokine activity and neuronal circuits mediating cognition and mood. Based on the neuroinflammation hypothesis, they would have the potential to prevent depression or anxiety or ameliorate symptoms in people already affected by these disorders.

These and other forms of neuromodulation might prevent the pathogenesis of full-blown psychiatric and neurological disorders and post-viral syndromes. But their immunomodulating effects could not suppress immunogenic mechanisms too much. If there was suppression, then it could disrupt the natural inflammatory response of microglia and cytokines to pathogens that had entered the brain. Failure to eliminate infectious agents due to an inadequate inflammatory response could result in as much neuronal damage as would have resulted from excess synaptic pruning or hyperinflammation. On the other hand, some molecules that otherwise would be tolerated in the brain may be mistaken by cytokines as threats and induce a damaging response. Pro- and anti-inflammatory cytokines can have protective or deleterious effects on brain function. This may depend on the context of activity in the brain, and it is not clear how changes in this context could produce such different effects.[135]

The relationship between synaptic pruning and inflammation and the brain changes associated with psychiatric disorders is complex and not entirely understood. Nor is it clear whether or to what extent different therapeutic interventions in the brain could prevent or alter their pathogenesis. The safety and efficacy of interventions for neurodevelopmental disorders that targeted dysregulated microglial and cytokine activity could only be confirmed by randomized controlled clinical trials. Among the issues these trials would have to clarify is whether any agent administered through the BBB would be able to induce and maintain an optimal level of synaptic connectivity and neurotransmission for healthy brain development.

These interventions presumably would be offered to adolescents deemed at risk of developing a neuropsychiatric disorder. This assessment would be based on genetic and epigenetic factors and neuroimaging detecting high levels of microglia- and cytokine-induced inflammation before any behavioral evidence of a disorder. Andrew Miller and Charles Raison point out that "the greater the inflammatory response [in the brain] to a psychosocial stressor, the more probable the subject is to develop depression over the ensuing months."[136] They also point out that "inflammation has been associated with antidepressant non-responsiveness."[137] This is one indication for intervening with drugs targeting inflammatory mechanisms before the prodromal stage of MDD. Mature minors could consent to participate in a clinical trial testing one of these drugs if researchers determined that these subjects had a clear understanding of the design and goals of the trial.[138] Otherwise, their parents could give proxy consent for them to participate in this research.

Many parents would be reluctant to allow their child to participate in a trial and receive a psychoactive drug when they were asymptomatic and displayed no behavioral symptoms of a disorder. Being at risk of a neuropsychiatric disorder does not imply that one will in fact develop it. Some parents might refuse to do this because, for them, the potential harm would outweigh any potential benefit. They would not have a therapeutic misconception about the research if their child was asymptomatic. Their concern would not be generated by the possibility of their child being in the control arm of the trial but with the unknown effects of the active intervention that was being tested. This could result in too few research subjects to yield statistically significant data about the effects of the intervention. In cases of trials involving individuals who were symptomatic, they or their parents would have to weigh the potential of ameliorating symptoms against the risk of adverse effects on other brain functions. A decision to participate or allow participation may depend on the severity of symptoms and how they affect the individual's functional capacity and quality of life.

Researchers have an ethical obligation to provide a high level of protection for individuals participating in research on neuromodulating interventions. This would include only "people at *ultra high risk* of psychosis."[139] Some individuals with a risk associated with a psychiatric disorder may not develop it and could be unnecessarily exposed to an agent that caused permanent deleterious effects on brain function. A certain number of subjects in phase 1 trials would be necessary to establish the safety of such an intervention before phase 2, 3, and 4 trials could establish its efficacy. Healthy subjects are allowed to participate in phase 1 trials testing other experimental drugs for certain diseases with potential but not known benefits and some known risks. But the difference between these subjects and those at risk of schizophrenia who are asymptomatic or with prodromal symptoms, but no definitive diagnosis, is significant because of the potentially worse adverse effects in the brain, mind, and body from altering interacting neuroimmune functions.

Abraham Reichenberg and Josephine Mollon emphasize the uncertainty in estimating outcomes of preventive interventions for schizophrenia. "There is . . . considerable heterogeneity within clinical high-risk samples because studies have consistently observed that most high-risk individuals do not go on to develop clinical psychosis, and a substantial minority may even recover symptomatically and functionally. Future research should focus on understanding the neurocognitive and psychosocial factors that characterize non-converters, as well as those who recover."[140] Therapeutic or preventive interventions in adolescence targeting neuroimmune interaction in general, and synaptic pruning in particular, might not be indicated in many cases. These considerations also apply to the association between neuroinflammation and MDD. Again, anti-inflammatory interventions have not been very effective in controlling the pathophysiology and symptoms of schizophrenia. But some patients with unipolar and bipolar depression experience psychotic episodes. They may benefit from drugs that modulated inflammation causing neuronal dysregulation associated with psychosis and related symptoms.

Studies have shown reduced brain-derived neurotrophic factor (BDNF) and mRNA levels in certain brain regions of some patients with schizophrenia and other neurodevelopmental disorders.[141] The level of the BDNF protein correlates positively with neuronal activity and synaptic connectivity in the prefrontal cortex. Reduced levels of BDNF and mRNA have been associated with reduced volume and connectivity in this region. Theoretically, infusing BDNF into the brain of a patient with this and related brain abnormalities might stop disease progression by inducing neuroplastic and neurogenerative mechanisms. This in turn might restore normal neuronal and synaptic connectivity.

Biological and psychosocial factors can influence people's brains in different ways. These differences may go some way toward explaining variability in neurocognitive functions along the neuropsychiatric spectrum. Without a better understand of the complex causal relationships involved in brain development over the lifespan, some people who would not develop a psychiatric disorder could be harmed by a psychotropic drug that would alter brain function. It could impair rather than improve working memory and other cognitive functions necessary for reasoning and decision-making. Neuronal changes induced by psychoactive substances could be especially harmful if they were given during adolescence, when the brain is still developing. Given the relatively high rate of psychiatric disease onset during this period, the reasons for intervening in the brains of individuals showing dysregulated synaptic pruning or chronic neuroinflammation are understandable. But these reasons must be weighed against the potential harm in altering the brain to prevent a disease that might not develop.

More speculatively, certain interventions might stop or reverse inflammation from hyperactive microglia or other dysregulated immune modulators implicated in Alzheimer's disease (AD). Activated microglia express diverse phenotypes that interact with amyloid-beta and tau, the two proteins whose dysregulation has been associated with the neuropathology characteristic of this disease.[142] By infusing certain immunomodulating agents into the brain, "microglia could potentially be modulated at various points in the AD trajectory to either prevent or modify disease progression."[143] It is also possible that these agents could reverse the brain inflammation in multiple sclerosis and other autoimmune diseases involving the brain. As the name implies, immunomodulating drugs would be designed to prevent uncontrolled cell proliferation. Yet they would have to avoid suppression of natural inflammatory mechanisms that ordinarily protect the brain from infectious agents. The risk of this suppression may be an acceptable trade-off for the potential benefit of the intervention in cases of advanced neuropathology, though this would also depend on the risk of other neurological sequelae.

This type of intervention could be used to prevent neurodegenerative disease based on biomarkers of neuropathology. It would depend on the predictive value of these biomarkers in asymptomatic individuals. As with individuals at risk of a neurodevelopmental disorder like schizophrenia, neurointerventions in individuals with biomarkers for a neurodegenerative disorder they would not develop could have deleterious effects in the brain.[144] In cases of neuroinflammation correlating with extensive neurodegeneration, attempts to modulate it and slow or stop disease progression may not be successful. In cases of neuroinflammation correlating with mild or moderate neurodegeneration, these attempts may be successful to some extent. Immunomodulating drugs might also mitigate the microglia-, cytokine-, and chemokine-induced inflammation in long COVID and ME/CFS.

It is important to emphasize that many of the interventions I have described are hypothetical. Controlled clinical trials would be necessary to determine their safety and efficacy. Cognitive impairment from a neuroinflammatory disorder would not likely preclude the capacity to give informed consent to participate in a trial testing an experimental treatment for it. Individuals with advanced neurodegenerative disease may lack this capacity. Family members could give proxy consent for them, though this assumes that a substitute decision was what the patient would have wanted and was in their best interests. Because of the disease and questions about their mental capacity, they would be vulnerable subjects who would need greater protection from researchers testing unproven therapies than those who were competent and at an earlier disease stage.[145] Uncertainty about potential benefit and risk of neurointerventions for asymptomatic and symptomatic patients who might develop or who have neurodevelopmental or neurodegenerative disorders underscores the importance of preventing them. This requires a better understanding of how biological and psychosocial factors influence neuro-immune interaction, and how they can cause this interaction to become dysregulated. This could go some way toward reducing the burden of these disorders on the people affected by them.

7 Immune and Genome Engineering

Advances in genome engineering targeting the immune system have shown the therapeutic potential of interventions at the intersection of immunology and genetics. One especially significant advance has been gene editing in the form of CRISPR (clustered regularly interspaced short palindromic repeats) Cas9 (CRISPR-associated protein 9). This is an endonuclease that causes a double-stranded DNA break allowing genome modification.[146] CRISPR developed from research on bacterial immune systems. This technique could be used to restore or regulate dysregulated immune functions.

Gene editing may involve deleting, altering, or inserting genes and their products whose presence or absence is associated with monogenic diseases. In the first therapeutic application of the technique in two patients with auto-somal recessive sickle cell disease and beta-thalassemia, researchers used CRISPR to correct a mutation in the beta-globin gene (BCL11A transcription factor) that represses hemoglobin in red blood cells. The gene was corrected in both patients through autologous stem cell transplantation using hematopoietic stem and progenitor cells from healthy donors. The technique resulted in increased hemoglobin levels, transfusion independence, and the elimination of vaso-occlusive episodes.[147]

Gene editing would be a critical component of regenerative immunology. Altering genes regulating immune cells and proteins could promote regeneration of tissues and organs damaged from hyperactive immune responses to pathogens.[148] In addition, tissue-engineered grafts could induce endogenous repair mechanisms in failing organs and thus obviate the need for organ transplantation.[149] This is an example of how the immune system does not only have a defensive function but also a regenerative and restorative one. This type of engineering would have to be controlled to prevent deleterious cell proliferation. Currently, it is not clear to what extent researchers would have this control in editing genes and immunity.

Innate and adaptive immunity protect us from pathogens. In doing this, though, they prevent the body from accepting tissues and organs transplanted from other organisms. Immunosuppressive drugs such as tacrolimus and siro-limus prevent acute rejection of allografts. Yet by suppressing immunogenic mechanisms, they can make a transplant recipient susceptible to infectious disease by weakening humoral and cellular responses to foreign antigens. Retinoic acid, dexamethasone, and dendritic cell-mediated nanomedicines can modulate immune responses to microbes and prevent autoimmune disease. Similarly, genetically engineered drugs that are tolerogenic rather than immunosuppressive can modulate T and B cell and antibody responses to the HLA antigen in transplanted tissues and organs. This may allow the acceptance of these grafts without compromising natural immunity. Because the drugs would not suppress but modulate these responses, a transplant recipient would not be as susceptible to opportunistic infections. But these drugs would be nonspecific. Their immunomodulatory properties potentially could still weaken innate and adaptive responses to some foreign antigens and directly or indirectly cause disease. If they disabled tumor suppressor genes, then they might allow proliferation of abnormal cells in neoplasms that could be cancerous.

Editing specific genes coding for proteins associated with MHC and HLA in donor tissue could prevent graft rejection and avoid off-target adverse effects in human-to-human and animal-to-human transplantation. The editing would delete or neutralize the antigen triggering acute hyperactive humoral and cellular responses to ensure graft survival. In addition, gene editing might be used to optimize humoral and cellular function to prevent us from contracting infectious diseases. This editing could ensure that natural antibodies and those generated by T and B cell and antibody responses to foreign antigens always neutralized them. It could also prevent antibodies from becoming autoreactive and destroying healthy cells, tissues, and organs. The editing must be highly specific, however. Off-target editing of genes regulating immune and other systemic functions could result in disease in people whose genes were edited. Even if the editing were gene-specific, it is not known whether altering dysregulated components of the immune system would alter regulated components or leave them intact. It is not known whether attempts to manipulate the immune system to restore or maintain homeostasis would always have positive effects. If it had the requisite level of specificity, then gene editing in transplantation, infectious disease, and autoimmune disease could optimize immune function to prevent harm from dysregulated immunity and benefit people by increasing their life expectancy and improving their functional capacity.

7.1 Immune and Genome Engineering in Xenotransplantation

In the United States alone, there are currently more than 100,000 people with end-stage organ disease waiting for an organ transplant.[150] Twenty-two people die each day waiting for what would have been a lifesaving intervention. This is due to the shortage of transplantable organs and tissues from deceased and living human donors. As noted, gene editing of MHC in allografts from human donors might prevent acute immune rejection in human transplant recipients. Still, it would not solve the problem of the availability of organs and tissues for all who need them. A potential solution to the problem of the shortage of sources for tissue and organ replacement would be animal-to-human transplantation. Advances in genetic engineering and immunological treatments are necessary to achieve this goal.

"Xenotransplantation has the potential to overcome the barriers of human allograft transplantation, such as donor-tissue availability and preservation."[151] Currently, "clinical applications of xenotransplantation primarily involve the use of a xenogeneic extracellular matrix rather than intact xenogeneic cells or tissues, because intact material induces strong adaptive and innate immune responses as a result of xenogeneic major histocompatibility complex (MHC), other membrane proteins, and glycans."[152] The natural immune response to xenografts is stronger than it is to allografts because the antigens are recognized as even more foreign to the recipient's immune system. But the use of extracellular matrices could overcome the currently intractable problem of hyperacute rejection of xenografts by innate and adaptive responses to them. These structures "are now known to have strong immunomodulatory properties that favor constructive tissue and organ remodeling."[153] Their immunomodulatory properties could regulate immunogenic properties of adaptive and innate immunity. This same effect could be produced by genetic modification of pigs so that intact tissues and organs from them would prevent rejection and allow successful transplantation from animals to humans. The main challenge is preventing a natural adaptive immune response to foreign antigens.

A porcine-to-human cardiac xenotransplantation involving gene-edited immunity was performed at the University of Maryland School of Medicine in June 2022.[154] A fifty-seven-year-old man with cardiomyopathy and other conditions was hospitalized for severe heart failure. He had multiple ventricular arrythmias causing cardiac arrest and was resuscitated. Because of his history of poor adherence to treatment and his biventricular heart failure, a request for a heart transplant was denied by four transplant programs. The transplant selection committee then considered the patient for experimental xenotransplantation. The hospital ethics committee determined that he had the capacity to consent to the transplant, the institutional review board approved the procedure, and the patient provided written informed consent to proceed.

Arguably, the patient's short life expectancy without an allograft made the potential benefit of living longer with a xenograft outweigh the risk of dying from complications of the procedure. The patient's nonadherence to medication was noted in the pre-transplant evaluation. This could complicate measures to ensure graft survival. Gene editing would not obviate the need for post-transplant immunosuppression because normal adaptive immunity rejecting the foreign antigen would likely develop four to seven days after exposure to the xenograft.[155] This would have to be mentioned in the information presented to the patient. The issue of adherence to medication following transplants in general and xenotransplants in particular underscores the need for psychosocial support of patients before and after transplantation.[156]

As an experimental procedure, the transplant could be defended as research designed to gain knowledge of physiological processes and outcomes of tissue and organ replacement from animals to humans. Nevertheless, controlled clinical trials will be necessary to establish the medical safety and efficacy as well as the ethical permissibility of xenotransplantation for it to become approved therapy for patients in end-stage organ failure. There will be medical and ethical challenges pertaining to both human and nonhuman animals in designing and completing these trials. A better understanding of gene-immune interaction is critical for the feasibility and acceptability of xenotransplantation.

The pig in this case was derived from fibroblasts and had a cell line of ten gene edits.[157] These edits included knocking out certain xenoantigens, as well as a growth hormone receptor, to limit xenograft growth beyond the targeted cardiovascular area. In addition to the gene editing, the patient received immunosuppressive drugs (KPL-404) immediately after the transplant to deplete peripheral B (CD20+) and T (CD3+) cells. This indicates that gene editing alone is not sufficient but must be supplemented by standard therapies to prevent xenograft rejection. The patient also received antiviral and antifungal prophylaxis.

On day 34, the xenograft was functioning normally without any evidence of rejection, and the patient did not need any cardiovascular support. On day 43, the patient's condition deteriorated, and he tested positive for porcine cytomegalovirus (pCMV). Physicians changed his antiviral therapy from ganciclovir to cidofovir.[158] Significantly, this porcine viral pathogen was not detected in the pre-transplant screening of the animal. On day 50, there was no evidence of antibody or cell-mediated rejection. But there were infiltrates in his lungs and other physiological processes that led to graft failure. His condition deteriorated. Sixty days after the transplant, life support was discontinued, and he died. Graft failure was not likely caused by the antibody and cellular responses to the genetically modified xenograft. More likely, it was a complication of cross-reactivity between the pCMV and a human herpes virus in the patient.[159]

Even if gene editing could prevent the immune system from rejecting foreign tissue without the need for immunosuppression, it may not be enough to ensure successful xenotransplantation. This case illustrates that hyperacute rejection of a xenograft is not the only obstacle to using animals for tissue and organ replacement in humans. Tissues from animals also often have foreign antigens associated with infectious agents. There may be transmission of a zoonotic disease that can not only destroy the graft but also result in multi-organ failure and death of the transplant recipient. These agents may not be detected by microbial analysis of animal tissue before transplantation. There was no evidence in the porcine-to-human heart transplant that editing genes to prevent rejection of the xenograft made the patient susceptible to the pCMV. In cases where these foreign antigens are not detected, successful xenotransplantation may require both: (1) editing of genes and their antigen products in foreign tissue; and either (2) editing genes to eliminate or neutralize pathogens in porcine cells; or (3) editing genes in human recipient cells to prevent them from exposure to pathogens. The third type of editing would not occur ex vivo in an extracellular matrix but in vivo in the recipient's own somatic cells. This may be a more challenging form of editing, and it raises more biological and ethical questions than the first and second types. Before discussing these questions, though, I will consider some ethical issues pertinent to xenotransplantation itself.

The case that I have just discussed involves two ethical issues concerning risk. The first is the risk of graft rejection and how this could harm the patient by not reversing end-stage organ disease. This would be in addition to the harm he experienced from heart disease and would add to his suffering. It could be worse than dying earlier from organ failure if the failed xenotransplant defeated the patient's expectation that the transplant would extend his life. The second is the risk of contracting a viral, bacterial, or fungal infection from the animal source of the tissue or organ. It could undermine the benefit from the recipient's immune system tolerating and accepting the xenograft. This risk is not unique to xenotransplantation, as some human recipients of allografts have contracted infections from transplanted tissue. But the risk is greater in animal-to-human organ and tissue replacement because it is more difficult to screen for infectious agents in animal tissue. Moreover, it may be more difficult for the B and T cells and antibodies in adaptive immunity to recognize and respond to foreign antigens associated with pathogens from animals than from humans because of molecular differences between human and nonhuman antigens. These pathogens may present a threat to the organism that its immune system cannot overcome.

Gene editing could reduce or eliminate the risk of adaptive immune rejection of xenografts by knocking out foreign antigens that would induce hyperacute rejection. It is not clear that CRISPR-Cas9 or other forms of editing could also prevent the transmission of pathogens from animals destroying these grafts or causing zoonotic disease. Improved methods of detecting infectious agents in animal tissue would be necessary to determine when gene editing would be appropriate. But the key issue is whether gene editing could eliminate, neutralize, or prevent human infection from these pathogens. It could mean altering millions of years of the evolution of microbes.

Earlier xenotransplantation research used monkeys and chimpanzees as organ sources. The United States Food and Drug Administration (FDA) banned the use of primates for this purpose in 1999, citing the high risk of zoonotic infection from them.[160] This was before the use of CRISPR Cas-9, which has increased the potential of xenotransplantation to become clinically available in the foreseeable future. Currently, "xenotransplantation remains experimental, and potential recipients of xenografts are research subjects whose consent and safety are governed by human subjects research regulations and guidance."[161] This includes "extended, possibly lifelong surveillance for zoonotic infectious diseases. The United States Public Health Service calls for lifelong surveillance of recipients to monitor for infectious agents and unexplained illness."[162] The United Kingdom's Nuffield Council on Bioethics has recommended that this monitoring be extended to family and close contacts of transplant recipients This would be included in the patient's consent, which would not be limited to the transplant itself but would extend over a long period after the transplant.

Syd Johnson raises ethical concerns about using pigs to grow transplantable organs. "While pigs are often farmed and killed in high numbers for human meat consumption, if they are used for multiple tissue and organ transplants, they could be subjected to repeated surgeries, causing pain and distress in these highly intelligent and social animals ... Further, using pigs or nonhuman primates for xenotransplantation research, or to grow organs, violates established best practices for animal care and welfare, which include providing ethologically appropriate environments that meet the animals' behavioral and physiological needs."[163]

Leaving these issues aside (if indeed they can be left aside), xenotransplantation could be ethically justified as an experimental procedure if a person in organ failure with only weeks or days to live did not have timely access to an organ from a human donor. If a competent patient knowing the potential benefit and risk of xenotransplantation gave informed consent to receive a heart or other organ from a pig or other animal, and consented to post-transplant monitoring, and if a hospital institutional review board approved the procedure, then it would be permissible to proceed with the xenotransplant.

Endogenous tissue regeneration through genetically engineering the immune system's own cells and proteins could restore organ function without allotransplantation or xenotransplantation. This would avoid the risk of graft rejection as well as the risk of transmitting infectious disease from donors to recipients. It would also avoid ethical issues surrounding the use of pigs or other animals as organ sources. Immune and tissue engineering could prevent the harm that patients in end-stage organ disease experience from failed transplantation or from not receiving a transplant. This research is still at an early stage, however. It will be some time before engineering the immune system in this way becomes a safe and effective practice with broad clinical applications and beneficial outcomes.

7.2 Gene Editing to Prevent Infectious Disease

Gene editing may make it possible to not only prevent transmission of infectious agents from xenografts but also and more generally to prevent humans from being infected by many or most pathogens and the diseases associated with them. In 2012, George Church and Edward Regis considered the potential to prevent viruses from causing debilitating disease and ending our lives. "One of the greatest human health innovations of all time would be to make ourselves multi-virus resistant – render ourselves immune to all viruses, known or unknown, whether current or waiting in the wings."[164] Presumably, Church and Regis are not literally referring to all viruses, but to those that could overwhelm the human immune system. These would include the H1N1 virus associated with the 1918 influenza pandemic, SARS-CoV-2, Ebola, measles, the adenovirus implicated in reported cases of childhood hepatitis in 2022, and the pCMV that affected the recipient of the pig heart xenotransplant, among others. The intervention would not prevent viruses or other microbes from entering the body but would enable the immune system to eliminate or neutralize them. While the authors describe this innovation as hypothetical, they could cite genome editing as the most promising means of achieving this goal. They could mention CRISPR gene editing as the most effective way of optimizing humoral and cellular immunity to protect us from the threat of viral and other pathogens. Their comment about viruses "waiting in the wings" refers to those that are unknown and could affect humans. We do not know what their genetic properties would be, how innate and adaptive immunity would respond to them, or whether they would be the source of future pandemics.

This raises the question of what the most effective and safest form of gene editing would be to prevent human susceptibility to viruses. Somatic cell gene editing (SCGE) would alter an individual's body cells. The changes in cell function would be limited to the recipient of the editing and not passed on to offspring. The editing could occur at different stages of a person's life and could protect them from viral, bacterial, or fungal infections, or diseases like cancer. It would be a prophylactic intervention. People would not need a vaccine to be protected from microbial threats. Germline gene editing (GGE) would be performed in the gametes, before a person existed, and would prevent them from contracting infectious diseases over the course of their lives. If this procedure were performed not only individually but also collectively, then it could have a significant impact on public health. Indeed, the effects of editing genes in one embryo would also be collective because they would be passed on to offspring. Another ethically significant difference between somatic cell and germline gene editing is that people who would be affected by the first intervention could consent to it while those affected by the second intervention could not. Their parents would consent to altering their genes. They would have to live with the consequences of an intervention that they could not decide to have and, depending on its effects, may not always be in their best interests.

Because GGE is still at an early experimental stage, it is not known whether its effects on the body in general and the immune system in particular would always be beneficial, or whether any harmful effects would be reversible. In 2015, the United Nations Educational, Scientific, and Cultural Organization's (UNESCO) International Bioethics Committee called for a moratorium on heritable genome editing for "at least as long as the safety and efficacy of the procedures are not adequately proven as treatments."[165] In its report on heritable genome editing in 2018, the Nuffield Council on Bioethics stated that this practice could be morally permissible in certain cases, including some forms of human enhancement.[166] In 2019, the World Health Organization (WHO) Expert Advisory Committee on Governance and Oversight of Human Genome Editing recommended adopting a moratorium on the use of this technique until further research established its long-term safety and efficacy.[167] This more cautionary position reflects the uncertainty of the effects of manipulating the human genome. Some bioethicists have argued that "there is a strong case for pursuing GGE for the prevention of disease."[168] The potential of GGE to prevent cancer and other diseases overrides objections to its use based on concern about unknown possible negative future effects. Some have argued that the moral implications of the collective harm from disease, and the potential of GGE to prevent it, make it not only permissible but obligatory to proceed with research and subsequent clinical applications.[169]

But the uncertainty of long-term effects of GGE support at most a weaker permissibility argument rather than a stronger obligatory argument for it. It is permissible when guided by a precautionary principle that places greater weight on avoiding long-term harm than on producing short-term benefit.[170] Assuming that the technique will be proven effective, the magnitude of the harm from infectious agents, cancer, and hereditary immune system disorders to people who exist now and those who will exist in the future provides a strong reason for GGE. Nevertheless, the potential harm from unintended adverse irreversible effects of GGE is also morally significant, especially if the technique were used on a collective scale and had effects on a large number of people. This could support a more conservative precautionary principle consistent with the WHO recommendation for a moratorium on GGE until there is a better understanding of its long-term effects. Research providing this understanding would be necessary for any clinical applications to be medically and morally permissible.

Germline gene editing at the embryonic stage to modify the immune system from birth might enable it to neutralize or eliminate pathogens that otherwise would be highly virulent. It could be part of engineering humoral and cell-mediated responses that would always involve optimal levels of antibodies and T and B cells specific to each antigen they encounter. But the editing would have to be specific to genes regulating specific immune functions and not alter other genes regulating other functions. It would likely aim at increasing T cell production and maintaining B cell and antibody production at certain levels over the person's lifespan. This assumes that the editing could control antigenic variation. As previously mentioned, this is the mechanism by which an infectious agent evolves by altering the proteins on its surface to avoid a host immune response. It generates mutations that can evade recognition of the antigen expressed by the infectious agent and limit or preclude an adaptive immune response. It is not known whether editing genes regulating humoral and cell-mediated immunity would always recognize and neutralize foreign antigens expressed by pathogens. Nor is it known whether or how genetically manipulating the production of neutralizing antibodies and T and B cells would influence macrophages and protein molecules such as cytokines mediating the inflammatory response to infectious agents.

Another question is whether gene editing could prevent immune imprinting.[171] This is the process through which initial exposure to a virus can limit or prevent B cells from producing enough neutralizing antibodies against new strains or variants of the virus, or against a new virus. Knocking out genes regulating memory T and B cells of the antigen expressed in the initial strain may be one way of avoiding imprinting. But it could also impair the adaptive response to other antigens expressed on other infectious agents.

It is not known whether gene editing that altered cells and antibodies in adaptive immunity would affect the balance between pro-inflammatory cytokines, such as IL-1, IL-6, and TNF-a, and anti-inflammatory cytokines, such as IL-10 and transforming growth factor beta (TGF-B), to prevent uncontrolled inflammation. Maintaining this balance is necessary to prevent a hyperactive inflammatory response in a cytokine storm resulting in damage to healthy cells, tissues, and organs. Again, this dysregulated immune response to a virus, rather than the virus itself, caused the high rates of mortality in the 1918 H1N1 pandemic and the early phases of the SARS-CoV-2 pandemic. Chronic hyper-inflammation has also been implicated in the neurological, psychological, and bodily sequelae of post-viral syndromes. Genetic manipulation would have to maintain homeostasis within the immune system. In addition to maintaining balance between the two types of cytokines, it would have to activate regulatory T lymphocytes to control autoreactive T lymphocytes and prevent them from attacking self-antigens and causing autoimmune diseases. Genetic manipulation would have to promote coordinated responses to pathogens from cells and proteins in innate and adaptive immunity. The long-term effects of what is still an experimental procedure are not known, But the possibility of adverse outcomes from altering genes regulating immunity cannot be dismissed out of hand.

One example of germline gene editing designed to make the immune system resistant to a virus was the 2018 experiment of scientist He Jiankui, who claimed to have created the world's first "CRISPR babies."[172] He edited the CCR5 gene in the germline of two embryos. CCR5 is a major receptor through which the human immunodeficiency virus (HIV) can infiltrate T cells. His hypothesis was that he could confer lifetime resistance to HIV by editing this gene and making these cells resistant to the virus and allowing other humoral and cell-mediated mechanisms to neutralize it. The consent process between this researcher and the parents of the embryos was flawed because he misleadingly described his experiment as "an AIDS vaccine development project."[173] There were no obvious clinical indications for the experiment. Another medically and ethically controversial feature of He's gene editing of the embryos was uncertainty about the effects of knocking out the CCR5 gene. While it might prevent HIV, altering genes might also make the people who developed from the embryos susceptible to pathogens such as the West Nile virus and influenza.[174] The potential positive and negative on- and off-target effects of editing genes regulating immune functions are unpredictable. This supports a precautionary principle in proceeding slowly with the research. It underscores the need for clinical trials to determine the safety and efficacy of the technique for different diseases and immune disorders.

These trials would not answer questions about the long-term effects of GGE. This would make it unclear when any prohibition or moratorium on GGE could end and when clinical applications could begin. Lisa Rosenbaum comments: "He's behavior has forced a reckoning within the scientific community, leading many observers to call for an international consensus to explicitly detail the circumstances under which clinical trials should be permitted. As [CRISPR discoverer Jennifer] Doudna remarks, however, perhaps the silver lining of this moment is that we have been pushed to confront, publicly, globally, and rather urgently, some of the thorny issues raised by germline editing research."[175] There is currently no such consensus on this research or how it should be used to alter immune functions.

A particularly morally problematic issue in germline genetic modification is that the future people whose lives would be affected by it do not yet exist. They cannot participate in public debate and cannot influence scientists on whether or how to use it. This is related to the issue of consent. Future people could benefit from or be harmed by editing and its effect on immune and other bodily systems. Yet they would have no role in establishing the conditions under which it would be permissible or impermissible. We cannot predict how gene editing would affect people in the distant future. Climate change and epigenetic factors influenced by it would mean that their environment could be very different from our own. These factors could have a significant impact on the human immune system and its ability to maintain homeostasis and protect organisms from pathogens. We cannot confidently claim that germline genome editing would make future people resistant to all or most infectious agents. This is a transgenerational problem of actions and their unknown consequences. Any adverse events of GGE could be inherited long after the genes were edited. They could extend over generations.

Genetic variants that have evolved to protect us from some diseases can make us susceptible to others. Regarding the Black Death of 1346–50, "the high mortality rate suggests that genetic variants that conferred protection against *Y. pestis* might have been under strong selection during this time."[176] The allele that has evolved from this pandemic and protects populations from the bacterium that caused it is also associated with increased susceptibility to autoimmune diseases. An allele selected to protect us from an infectious disease may cause dysregulation in the immune system itself. Depending on epigenetic processes in the interaction between human organisms and the environment, editing genes to protect us from one or more diseases could have untoward effects on immunity.

Parents of embryos could give informed consent to a technique that could end heritable diseases. But the informed aspect of their consent would be limited given the uncertainty about effects extending well into the future. It is important to emphasize that people who develop from these embryos and whose immune systems would be altered by GGE could not consent to changes in the genotypic and phenotypic traits that could shape many dimensions of their lives. The moral issue is not that gene editing might alter a person's identity but that people whose genes, or whose ancestors' genes, were edited could be positively or negatively affected by actions beyond their control.

Even if GGE research in principle could meet all medical and ethical requirements for safety and efficacy, and even if the information people received about it was accurate, it would be difficult to reach scientific and social consensus on whether or how to proceed with this intervention. The different recommendations of the Nuffield Council on Bioethics, the UNESCO International Bioethics Committee, and the WHO Expert Advisory Committee, and disagreement among scientists about the pace at which gene editing should proceed, raise questions about the prospects of reaching consensus.[177] Professional disagreement could generate public disagreement and distrust of the technique and the scientists using it. Many people would worry that scientists would not be able to correct any deleterious effects of editing that would be passed on to future generations. Some would be averse to the idea of tinkering with genes regulating immune function. Others, citing the potential of GGE to protect us from infectious agents, would argue in favor of using it. They could argue that GGE would offer greater protection against diseases than vaccines. Different attitudes about altering genes at the germline raise serious questions about the likelihood of consensus on this issue.

In Section 4, I noted that, as of mid-2022, vaccines for SARS-CoV-2 had saved an estimated 20 million lives globally. Programming the immune system to neutralize or eliminate all pathogens could save many more. While this prospect would be welcomed by some, the unknown transgenerational effects of germline genetic alteration of immunity might instill fear and anxiety in others. Those unconcerned about future generations would be indifferent or not give much thought to the potentially beneficial or harmful temporally distant consequences of modifying the germline. In light of the reaction from some segments of society to COVID-19 vaccine mandates as a violation of individual liberty, there would likely be strong opposition to mandating or even recommending GGE in many jurisdictions. The health innovation mentioned by Church and Regis might not even get off the ground.

SCGE using CRISPR is less medically and morally controversial than GGE. Any harmful effects from the technique would be limited to the person for whom it was used. It would not be inherited by offspring. Unlike GGE, potential recipients of SCGE who were competent and understood the benefits and risks of the procedure could decide to accept or refuse it. In addition to sickle cell disease and beta-thalassemia, somatic cell gene editing has been used experimentally for more than twenty years to treat Mendelian disorders such as X-linked severe combined immune deficiency (SCID-X1). Most patients receiving these interventions are children incapable of consenting to them. Their parents consent for them. What distinguishes SCGE from GGE in this context is that the children are affected by life-threatening diseases without any therapeutic alternatives. But here too there are questions about unintended and unwanted consequences. Inserting genes into somatic cells to generate and maintain immune function could deactivate genes controlling cell growth and proliferation. They might deactivate tumor suppressor genes and activate oncogenes leading to cancer.

Consider the 2002 experimental gene therapy trials in France for boys with SCID-X1. Parental consent to SCGE was not an ethical issue because of the severity of the disorder and lack of alternative therapies. Several of the subjects whose genes were manipulated with a retroviral vector subsequently developed leukemia.[178] The successful intervention to reverse the dysregulated T lymphocyte differentiation and depletion characteristic of the disease appeared to disrupt the production of NK and CD8+ T cells that ordinarily would have suppressed cancer cells in the blood. This is one case illustrating that therapeutic gene editing may not always have beneficial outcomes. CRISPR involves a different mechanism from earlier experimental forms of gene therapy, which, like the SCID-X1 trials, used viral vectors. But this does not eliminate the possibility of adverse effects when the technique is used to alter genes in somatic cells regulating immune functions.

This is one of the risks associated with somatic cell gene editing. Unlike germline gene editing, though, this risk would be considered by individuals consenting, or their parents consenting, to undergo a procedure tested in clinical trials and proven to control a severe disease. The procedure has known benefits. Moreover, clinical trials testing SCGE, like the one for SCID-X1, are more medically and ethically acceptable than experiments testing GGE because the effects of the intervention can be observed within a shorter period.

Eli Adashi and Ivan Glenn Cohen point out that "somatic enhancement of passive immunity by way of monoclonal or polyclonal antibodies" could be an alternative to current vaccines or antiviral drugs for SARS-CoV-2.[179] Monoclonal antibodies are created by cloning a unique white cell line within the body. They are epitope-specific in binding to a single segment of antigen. Polyclonal antibodies are produced by different B cell clones. They are non-epitope- specific in binding to multiple segments of antigen. Adashi and Cohen note that "pandemics are an evolutionary inevitability because random mutations transform otherwise harmless life forms into potent pathogens, a threat for which the adaptive immune system is far too slow to counter."[180] The type of immune enhancement they describe could counter this threat. They cite a study in which "primary human B lymphocytes were CRISPR-edited to yield polyclonal antibodies aimed at several viral threats."[181] And "in one highly publicized case, potent human monoclonal antibodies effectively countered symptomatic Ebola virus infections."[182] Monoclonal antibodies have been used effectively to control malaria in Mali.[183] While acknowledging the need for intermittent replacement of these antibodies and the early stage of the research, Adashi and Cohen state that "autologous genetically engineered T lymphocytes revolutionized the care of cancer" (p. 83). I discussed this in Section 5 on immuno-oncology. The same type of genetic engineering could be used to optimize cell-mediated immunity to control viruses. "Reliance on such CRISPR-edited cellular therapeutics for the treatment of acutely ill patients with SARS-CoV-2 is just a matter of time."[184] Further research and clinical application of these therapeutics will determine how effective they are against this and other infectious agents.

CRISPR-edited cellular therapeutics could strengthen adaptive immunity by optimizing production of B and T lymphocytes to treat symptomatic viral infections. Could this editing of somatic cells prevent people from becoming infected? This assumes that polyclonal antibodies and activated T lymphocytes would be able to recognize and respond to all random mutations in a virus. Memory T and B cells would not recognize these mutations if they had not encountered them before. Variations in antigens expressed by a virus as it mutates could prevent immunological memory of an antigen that could evade a humoral and cell-mediated response. One cannot assume that SCGE of adaptive immunity could program immunological memory to always recognize and effectively respond to an antigen that posed an immediate threat to an organism at a specific time. As the high rate of mortality among adults infected by the 1889–1890 H3N8 and the 1918 H1N1 viruses illustrates, the immunological memory of a more remotely encountered antigen could override the memory of a more recently encountered antigen and weaken the adaptive response to the latter. T and B cell production would not necessarily provide greater protection against a virus because these cells might not recognize the antigen to which immunological memory was primed. It is unclear whether somatic cell gene editing of adaptive immunity could always ensure an optimal response to all pathogens.

Somatic-cell genetic modification of immunity to treat or prevent infectious disease would likely be expensive and not covered by many health care systems. This would be the case even if it transitioned from experimental to approved therapy. Only those with the financial means could pay for it. It raises questions about fairness in access to potentially therapeutic or preventive interventions. The inequality in access to this technique and health outcomes, with some people being protected from infectious diseases, and others being susceptible to them, would seem unfair when all had the same goal of avoiding infection and the resulting disease, disability, and death. Nevertheless, unequal access to this intervention would be unfair only if it were safe and effective. This has yet to be determined. Claims about unfair access and outcomes can only be confirmed or disconfirmed by data from further research and clinical applications.

8 Conclusion: Immunity, Microbes, and Humans

In a 1988 essay on pandemics, Nobel laureate Joshua Lederberg wrote:

> In the normal immune-competent individual, each incipient infection is a mortal race between the penetration and proliferation of the virus within the

body, and the development of antibodies that will dampen or extinguish the infection. If we have been vaccinated or infected before with a virus related to the current infection, we can mobilize an early immune response. But this, in turn, provides selective pressure on virus populations, encouraging the emergence of antigenic variants . . . We have no guarantee that the natural evolutionary competition of viruses with the human species will always find ourselves the winner.[185]

When Lederberg wrote these words, HIV had already taken more than 100,000 lives globally. Although there still is no vaccine for this virus, the advent of antiretroviral drugs in the 1990s and their continued ability to control the rate of viral replication and maintain adequate counts of antigen-specific CD4+ T cells in the body have allowed us to stay one step ahead of it. In the future, one or more pathogens may emerge that no vaccine or drug can control. It is possible that the competition between us and pathogens would result in their favor and lead to our demise. Bacteria caused the great plagues of the past. Some bacterial, fungal, and other infections can be fatal. In more recent history, viruses have had the highest mortality rate among infectious agents and pose the greatest threat to our existence.

The more than 6.7 million deaths from SARS-CoV-2 as of January 2023 are an example of how virulent viruses can be. This virus is just one example of how infectious agents can jump from nonhuman animals to humans. The incidence of zoonotic diseases has been accelerated by an increase in interspecies interaction from deforestation and other environmental changes. Vaccine-induced immunity and infection-induced acquired immunity may weaken the virulence and limit the transmissibility of some viruses. This could result in herd immunity, where the number of people immune to the virus prevents its ability to transmit to new hosts. But the emergence of new viral variants, or a new virus, could prevent this. The ability of a virus to mutate can give it an evolutionary advantage over our immune responses to it.

In June 2022, data indicated that Omicron subvariants BA.4 and BA.5 of SARS-CoV-2 appeared to escape antibody responses in people who had had a previous infection and those who had been fully vaccinated with two inoculations plus a booster.[186] More recently, researchers reported that the BA.4.6 variant showed a greater ability to escape neutralizing antibodies induced by infection or a vaccine than previous variants.[187] Many researchers have advocated booster vaccines to protect against emerging variants of this virus.[188] Yet new variants and subvariants of a virus can emerge as it evolves. New variant lineages, such as the highly transmissible XBB.1.5 and BQ1.1 Omicron subvariants, may evade immunity more effectively than previous variants.[189] Bivalent vaccines target two or more new viral strains. But they may fail if immune imprinting primes the immune system to respond to epitopes of older strains rather than to epitopes of newer strains.[190]

Vaccines delivered intranasally may prevent viral transmission through nasal mucosa by preventing nasopharyngeal replication.[191] This would depend on the virus and the specificity of antibody-antigen binding. Vaccines that have prevented some infections from affecting humans could prevent others. For example, the BCG tuberculosis vaccine could protect against SARS-CoV-2. But it is not clear whether a vaccine effectively targeting one antigen would be equally effective in targeting another, or whether it would target the more virulent antigen. Researchers reported in September 2022 that certain recombinant antibodies in mouse models could broadly neutralize all severe acute respiratory syndrome coronavirus variants, including the Omicron subvariant BA.5.[192] It remains to be seen whether this result could be translated to humans. Antiviral drugs may prevent some viruses from replicating. But they will not prevent them from mutating.

Deep mutational scanning (DMS) has been used to identify SARS-CoV-2 in rapid antigen testing. This technique uses DNA sequencing to measure a large number of protein variants in viruses.[193] In the near or further future, advanced DMS could be used to predict the evolution of viruses and prepare vaccines against them. It could be part of somatic cell and possibly germline interventions to program people's immune systems to prevent viruses and other pathogens from causing disease and death. Again, though, epigenetic factors shaped by a natural environment changing at an accelerated pace could influence the evolution of pathogens and how our immune systems respond to them. DMS or other techniques could not influence the environmental sources of pathogens and may not prevent their deleterious effects on us. It is questionable whether these techniques could always prevent or mitigate the consequences of antigenic drift, antigenic shift, antigenic variation, and antigenic sin.

We cannot assume that humans will always control the evolution of viruses. It would be hubristic to make this assumption.[194] Vaccines may not always generate the level of acquired immunity necessary to prevent disease because they may not always keep pace with random genetic mutations in foreign antigens. Even a low viral load can lead to T-cell exhaustion from prolonged exposure and a prolonged adaptive response to these antigens. Spike proteins in coronaviruses could evolve through antigenic drift to escape recognition by memory T and B cells. Viral evolution could allow new variants in these and other pathogens to evade vaccines and become more infectious. Mutations can cause viruses to weaken. They might also allow them to evade innate and adaptive immune defenses. A universal coronavirus vaccine targeting all variants could control viral mutations and replication.[195] But coronaviruses are not the only class of viruses. Emerging viruses and other pathogens could threaten us. It is doubtful that a vaccine could be developed, or that genes could be edited, to prevent susceptibility to all pathogens. Even if gene editing could prevent infectious diseases, it could alter certain immune genes and make us more susceptible to autoimmune diseases. This reflects how evolution may select for different alleles associated with different diseases in different circumstances.

Although it may not be probable, it is possible that a pathogen could cause the extinction of the human species. This obviously would be bad for us by causing people to suffer and shortening their lives. In natural biological terms, extinction would be one possible amoral outcome of interaction between pathogens and humans. Claims to the contrary would reflect an anthropocentric view of nature. Microbes were around long before humans existed and will be around long after humans have disappeared from the earth.[196] While the process of becoming extinct would be bad for people who experienced its effects, a state of extinction would be neither good nor bad for anyone because no one would exist in such a state. Only people who exist now or who will exist in the future can have interests and benefit from or be harmed by events that affect them. Possible people who might have existed but will not actually exist do not have interests.[197] This includes an interest in coming into existence. They cannot benefit from or be harmed by any state of affairs. Specifically, they could not be harmed by not coming into existence if an infectious agent extinguished the human species. Extinction would be normatively neutral in this regard.[198]

Immunogenic and tolerogenic interventions can optimize immune functions to enable better control of cancer, reduce the incidence of autoimmune disease, and improve outcomes in allotransplantation and xenotransplantation. Vaccines can protect us to a considerable degree from infectious diseases. They may prevent infection or ensure that the agents that do infect us remain endemic and do not become epidemic or pandemic. Yet while these measures can reduce the risk of contracting disease, they cannot eliminate this risk. It is an unavoidable part of evolutionary biology. The thought that humans could lose in competition with one or more pathogens is distressing. Yet, as Lederberg noted, it is one possible outcome of humans sharing the planet with microbes, one that authors such as Church and Regis and, indeed, all of us cannot ignore.

Glossary

Adaptive Immunity   The evolutionarily more recent form of immunity involving a specific rather than generalized response to antigenic epitopes expressed by pathogens. It is composed of T and B cells and antibodies (produced by B cells). The hallmark of adaptive immunity is the ability of T and B cells to form a memory of an antigen when they encounter it, enabling a more effective cell and antibody response to the antigen on each subsequent encounter.

Allograft   A graft of cells or tissue from one individual member of a species to another.

Antibody   A protein in the blood produced by B cells in response to a specific antigen and capable of recognizing and promoting its elimination from the body.

Antigen   A molecule or part of a molecule that induces antibody production as a specific immune response to it. An antigen may be composed of different epitopes.

Antigenic Drift   The process in which there is an accumulation of genetic errors during viral replication.

Antigenic Shift   The process in which genetic recombination causes changes in the dominant antigen expressed by a virus.

Antigenic Sin   The immune system's tendency to preferentially respond to an antigen from a previous infection when a slightly different and more recent version of the antigen is encountered.

Antigenic Variation   The process in which a protozoan, bacterium, or virus evolves by altering the proteins on its surface to avoid a host immune response.

Autoantibody   An antibody produced and directed against an individual's own epitopes.

Autoreactivity   Immune activity directed against host self-antigens.

Autoimmune Disease   A disease characterized by inflammation and tissue injury from an autoreactive immune response.

B cells (B Lymphocytes)   With T cells, these are the main components of antigen-specific adaptive immunity. B cells produce antibodies.

Blood-Brain Barrier   A semi-permeable border of endothelial cells that prevents many molecules, including pathogens and toxic agents, from entering the brain.

Brain-Derived Neurotrophic Factor (BDNF)   A protein that regulates neuronal activity and synaptic connectivity.

Cell-Mediated (Cellular) Immunity   The form of adaptive immunity consisting of mature T cells.

Chemokine   A cytokine produced by one type of cell that attracts other cells to the same location.

Chimeric Antigen Receptor T Cell Therapy (CAR-T)   A type of immunotherapy involving genetically engineered T cells that target a cancer-specific antigen, CD19-CAR-T. The engineered cells have receptors that bind to and destroy cancer cells.

Complement   A series of proteins in the innate immune system that mediate immune functions such as inflammation, cell lysis, and tagging for phagocytosis.

CRISPR Cas9   Clustered regularly interspaced short palindromic repeats, and CRISPR-associated protein 9. This is an endonuclease that causes a double-stranded DNA break allowing genome modification.

Cytokines   Signaling protein molecules that enable immune cells to communicate with each other. They mediate inflammation in the body and brain They can be both pro-inflammatory (Interlcukin 1 and 6, Tumor Necrosis Factor-alpha) and anti-inflammatory (Interleukin 4, 10, and 13). They are produced by both innate and adaptive immune cells.

Cytokine Storm/Cytokine Release Syndrome   Any one of several disorders of immune dysregulation characterized by systemic inflammation and multi-organ dysfunction that may lead to multi-organ failure. They are triggered by excessive amounts of pro-inflammatory cytokines.

Deep Mutational Scanning   A technique using DNA sequencing to measure a large number of protein variants in viruses.

Dendritic Cell   A white blood cell of the innate immune system that senses microbes, releases inflammatory cytokines, and presents antigens to T cells.

Eosinophil   A type of while blood cell in the innate immune system that responds to infections.

Epitope   The specific part of an antigen to which an antibody binds.

Germline Gene Editing (GGE)   Altering specific genes of an egg, sperm cells, or early embryo. The effects of altering these genes are passed on to offspring.

Human Leukocyte Antigen (HLA)   A human version of MHC. It has a critical role in immune surveillance and the immune response to transplanted tissues and organs.

Humoral Immunity   The form of adaptive immunity mediated by antibodies.

Immune Checkpoint Inhibitors (ICIs) A type of immunotherapy that inhibits checkpoint proteins from binding with other proteins, including those on tumor cells. This prevents deactivation of T cells and allows them to destroy cancer cells.

Immune Imprinting The phenomenon whereby initial exposure to a virus can limit or prevent B cells from producing enough neutralizing antibodies against new strains or variants of the virus.

Immunogenic The ability of an antigen or other substance to induce an adaptive immune response from B and T cells and antibodies.

Immunoglobins A class of immune system proteins that function as antibodies.

Innate Immunity The evolutionarily older form of immunity involving a first-line generalized response to pathogens or other microbes without recognizing and responding to specific antigens.

Macrophages Innate immune cells critical for phagocytosis and cytokine activation. They can also activate or inhibit T cell production.

Major Histocompatibility Complex (MHC) A collection of genes controlling a range of immune functions. It regulates T cell responses to foreign tissue antigens as well as T cell autorecognition.

Microbes Bacteria, protozoa, fungi, viruses, and other microorganisms that may be beneficial or harmful to human organisms. Many microbes are not pathogenic but have a symbiotic relationship with immune and other bodily systems.

Microglia Specialized macrophage immune cells constituting 5–10 percent of all brain cells. Their main functions are to maintain CNS homeostasis and respond rapidly to infection in the brain.

Molecular Mimicry A type of immune response to an infectious agent involving a cross-reactive response to self-antigens with close molecular similarities to the infectious agent.

Monoclonal Antibody An antibody deriving from a single-cell precursor with a specific antigenic specificity

mRNA Vaccines Vaccines using messenger RNA to induce an immune response to an antigen expressed by an infectious agent.

Natural Killer (NK) Cell A white blood cell of the innate immune system involved in controlling cancer and viral infections.

Neuroinflammation Inflammation in the brain associated with hyperactive microglia and pro-inflammatory cytokines.

Neutrophils The most abundant type of white blood cell in the innate immune system, critical to the immune response to infectious agents.

Pathogen   Any organism that causes disease.

Phagocytes   Cells of the innate immune system that engulf, ingest, and degrade other cells (phagocytosis).

Polyclonal Antibody   An antibody deriving from different cell precursors with different antigenic specificities.

Self-Nonself Distinction in Immunology   The idea that cells and proteins internal to the immune system protect the organism, and that microbes and molecules external to the immune system threaten it. Immune tolerance of microbes and the foreign antigens they express, on the one hand, and pathogenic autoreactivity of self-antigens in autoimmune disease, on the other, are examples of how this distinction collapses.

Somatic Cell Gene Editing (SCGE)   Altering specific genes in an individual's body cells. The effects of the editing are not passed on to offspring.

T Cells (T lymphocytes)   These cells are the main component of cell-mediated adaptive immunity. They include CD4+ "helper" T cells and CD8+ "cytotoxic" T cells.

T Cell Exhaustion   Progressive loss of effector and memory capacity of T cells from persistent antigenic exposure. T cell responses to viral or tumor antigens become weaker from this exposure.

Tolerogenic   Capable of producing immune tolerance to antigens without a hyperacute rejection of or hyperinflammatory response to cells and tissues expressing antigens.

Xenograft   A graft of tissue from a donor to a recipient of a different species.

Xenotransplantation   The transplantation of tissues or organs from a donor to a recipient organism of a different species.

Zoonotic Diseases   Any group of diseases that are transmissible to humans from nonhuman vertebrate animals.

Notes

1. Janeway 2001; Frank 2002.
2. Burnet 1962;Pradeu 2020, 16; Alt 2020.
3. Pradeu, 2020, 6.
4. Pradeu 2012; Eberl 2016; Tauber 2017.
5. Pradeu 2020, 11.
6. Klunk et al 2022, 312; Green 2020.
7. Feinberg 1986; Arneson 2022.
8. Kant 1785/1964; Thomson 1990; O'Neill 2013.
9. Driver 2012.
10. Kamm 2007.
11. Scanlon 1998; Parfit 2011, volume 1, part 3.
12. Abbas, Lichtman, & Pillai 2018;Pradeu 2020, 5; Clark 2008, 3–13; Doan, Melvold, & Waltenbaugh 2005, 5.
13. Doan, Melvold, &Waltenbaugh 2005, 7.
14. Frank 2002, 22–32.
15. Francis 1960; Gagnon et al. 2013.
16. Gagnon et al. 2013, 6–7; 2015.
17. Gagnon et al. 2013, 5.
18. Klein 1982; Janeway 1992; Clark 2008; Tauber 1994 and 2017; Pradeu 2012 and 2020.
19. Abbas, Lichtman, & Pillai 2018, 193, 277, 317.
20. Fajgenbaum & June 2020, 2255.
21. Pradeu 2020, 6.
22. Ibid., 18.
23. Ibid., 18.
24. Ibid., 20.
25. For example, Anomaly 2020, chapter 4.
26. Juengst 1998, 29.
27. Harris 2007, 57.
28. For an optimizing view of enhancement, see Metzinger & Hildt 2011. For a maximizing view, see Bostrom & Sandberg 2009. While these authors focus mainly on cognitive enhancement, the idea of optimizing or maximizing can be applied to any type of function in an organism, including immune function.
29. Fajgenbaum & June 2020, 2256.
30. Ibid., 2256.
31. Burnet 1962;Pradeu 2020, 16.
32. Bluestone and Anderson 2020, 1156.
33. Schietinger 2022.
34. Guerriero 2019.
35. Huyghe et al. 2020.

36. Cifuentes-Rius, Desai, Yuen, et al. 2021.
37. Doan, Melvold, & Waltenbaugh 2005, 155.
38. Doan, Melvold, & Waltenbaugh 2005, 9.
39. Doan, Melvold, & Waltenbaugh 2005, 9.
40. Blank et al. 2019.
41. Bluestone and Anderson 2020, 1160.
42. Miao, Zhang, & Huang 2021.
43. https://covid19.who.int; https://coronavirus.jhu.edu/data; www.who.int/publications/m/item/weekly-epidemiological-update-on-Covid-19–11 January 2023 Accessed January 14, 2023.
44. Rogers & Lewis 2022; Venkataramani & Winkler 2022; Sivan et al. 2022.
45. www.cdc.gov/opioids/data/index/html Accessed October 18, 2022.
46. Pravetoni & Comer 2019; Volkow, Michaelides, & Baler 2019. https://cumc.columbia.edu/clinical_trial/2168.
47. Baker, Koroshetz, & Volkow 2021.
48. Heyman 2009, Cf. Volkow & Li 2004.
49. See, for example, McHugh, Hearon, & Otto 2010.
50. Young et al. 2012, p. 524.
51. Hall, Carter, & Forlini 2015; Young et al. 2012, p. 523.
52. Wertheimer 1987; Wertheimer & Miller 2014.
53. Thomson 1990; Driver 2012.
54. Young et al. 2012, 524.
55. Ibid., 523.
56. Ibid., 524.
57. Eyal 2020; Eyal, Caplan, & Plotkin 2021.
58. Eyal & Gerhard 2022.
59. Ibid., 588.
60. *BMJ*, Polio Vaccine Is Offered to All Children in London Ages 1 to 9 after Virus Detected in Sewage, 378 (2022):o2007. https://doi.10.1136/bmj.02007, August 11, 2022. Accessed August 11, 2022.
61. Beauchamp & Childress 2019, chapter 4.
62. Mina et al. 2019, 599.
63. Ibid., 599.
64. Ibid., 599.
65. Bester 2022, 158.
66. Hobbes 1651/2017; Gauthier 1986.
67. Kant 1785/1964; O'Neill 2013; Moran 2022.
68. Rousseau 1762/1997.
69. Scanlon 1998; Parfit 2011, volume 1, part 3.
70. Feinberg 1992.
71. Wilkinson 2022.
72. British Columbia Centre for Disease Control, September 14, 2022. www.bccdc.ca/health-info/diseases-conditions/covid-19
73. Kraaijeveld, Gur-Arie, & Jamrozik 2022.
74. Anderson et al. 2022.

75. He et al. 2022.
76. From JHU Coronavirus data. www.jhu.edu/data-covid-19. Accessed November 26, 2022.
77. Lin et al. 2022.
78. Opel, Diekema, & Ross 2021.
79. *Jacobson v. Massachusetts* 1905.
80. Mill 1859/1974, 69.
81. Mill 1859/1974, 68.
82. *Jacobson v. Massachusetts.*
83. Pugh et al. 2022.
84. Hermann, Lee, Balte, et al. 2022.
85. Daniels 2009; Rawls 1971.
86. Shaw 2022; Cf. Schuman, Robertson-Preidler, & Bibler 2022.
87. Arneson 2022; Adler & Norheim 2022; Brock 2012, Parfit 1997.
88. Kamm 2007, 14.
89. Arneson 2004.
90. Adler & Norheim 2022.
91. Parent, Caplan, & Mehta 2021, 2.
92. American Society of Transplant Surgeons, 2021, https://asts.org/advocacy/covid-19-resources/asts-covid-19-strike-force/transplant-caoacity-in-the-Covid-19-era#.YEKAXI1Kgc8. Accessed November 26, 2022; Pereira et al. 2020.
93. Cited by Parent, Caplan, & Mehta 2021, 2.
94. Parent, Caplan, & Mehta 2021, 3.
95. *CBC News*, Alberta Court of Appeal Rejects Unvaccinated Woman's Request to Get Back on Transplant List, November 8, 2022. www.cbc.ca/news/canada/edmonton/appeal-court-rejects-unvaccinated-woman-s-request-to-get-back-on-transplant-list Accessed November 8, 2022.
96. Pradeu 2020, 31.
97. Scherer, Babiker, Adelman, et al. 2022.
98. Beaver & Pazdur 2022.
99. Rohaan, Borch, van dem Berg, et al. 2022.
100. Shiravand, Khodadadi, Kashani, et al. 2022.
101. Mantia & Buchbinder 2019; Gumusay, Callan, & Rugo 2022; Hegle & Chen 2020.
102. Bao & Jiang 2022.
103. Schietinger 2022, 2334.
104. Ibid., 2334.
105. Melenhorst, Chen, Wang, et al. 2022
106. Guerriero 2019.
107. Huyghe et al. 2020.
108. Rohaan, Birch, van den Berg, et al. 2022.
109. Mathews, Fins, & Racine 2018.
110. Beauchamp & Childress 2019, chapters 5 & 6.
111. Beaver & Pazdur 2022, 1298.

112. Ibid., 1299.
113. Ibid., 1300
114. Ribeiro et al. 2022.
115. Talbot, Foster, & Woolf 2016, 422; Dantzer 2018; Pradeu 2018, 46ff.; Bullmore 2018
116. Beural, Toups, & Nemeroff 2020, 235.
117. Ibid., 235.
118. Bloomfield, Selvaraj, Veronese, et al. 2016.
119. Waltl & Kalinke 2022.
120. Muzio, Viotti, & Martino 2021.
121. Paus, Keshavan, & Giedd 2008; Keshavan, Giedd, Lau, et al. 2014.
122. Beurel, Toups, & Nemeroff 2020, 235.
123. Miller & Raison 2016, 27.
124. Ibid., 236.
125. Ibid., 236; Miller, Maletic, & Raison 2009; Miller & Raison 2016; Dantzer, O'Connor, Freund, et al. 2008.
126. Murphy, Walker & Weikert 2021.
127. Tate et al. 2022.
128. Venkataramani & Winkler 2022.
129. Ibid.
130. Beurel, Toups, & Nemeroff 2020; Vigo, Thornicroft, & Atun 2016.
131. Birnbaum & Weinberger 2020.
132. Howes & McCutcheon 2015.
133. Inta, Lang, Borgwardt, et al. 2017.
134. Sauder, Allen, Baker, et al 2022.
135. Beurel, Toups, & Nemeroff 2020, 236.
136. Miller & Raison 2016, 22.
137. Ibid., 25.
138. Beauchamp & Childress 2019, chapter 4; Emanuel, Grady, Crouch, et al. 2011.
139. Bloomfield, Selvaraj, Veronese, et al. 2016, 44; Beauchamp & Childress 2019, chapter 5.
140. Reichenberg & Mollon 2016, 1249–50.
141. Balu & Coyle 2011; Boksa 2012, 76.
142. Leng & Edison 2021, 157.
143. Ibid., 157.
144. Glannon 2022.
145. Beauchamp & Childress 2019, chapter 5.
146. Jinek et al. 2012; Hsu, Lander, & Zhang 2014; Cyranoski 2016; Doudna & Sternberg 2018.
147. Frangoul et al. 2021.
148. Elisseeff, Badylak, & Boeke 2021, 2451.
149. Ibid., p. 2453.
150. United Network of Organ Sharing (UNOS), https://unos.org.data/ Accessed October 15, 2022.

151. Elisseeff, Badylak, & Boeke 2021, 2451–2.
152. Ibid., 2453.
153. Ibid., 2452.
154. Griffith et al. 2022.
155. I thank transplant surgeon Dr. James Thisthlethwaite, and Dr. Lainie Friedman Ross, for this point.
156. Silverman & Odonkor 2022.
157. Griffith et al. 2022, 36.
158. Ibid., 39.
159. Ibid., 41; Fishman 2022.
160. Johnson 2022a, 2022b.
161. Johnson 2022a, 2.
162. Ibid., 2.
163. Ibid., 2.
164. Church & Regis 2012, 109.
165. Cited by Baylis 2019, 159ff.
166. Ibid.
167. Ibid.
168. Gyngell, Douglas, & Savulescu 2017, 498.
169. Gyngell, Bowman-Smart, & Savulescu 2019.
170. Koplin, Gyngell, & Savulescu 2020; Pugh et al. 2022.
171. Roltgen et al. 2022.
172. Lowe 2018.
173. Cited by Rosenbaum 2019, 971.
174. Rosenbaum 2019, 971.
175. Ibid., 971–2.
176. Klunk et al. 2022, 2.
177. Baylis 2019, chapter 8.
178. Check 2002; Edelstein, Abedi, & Wixon 2007; Hacein-Bey-Albina et al. 2008.
179. Adashi & Cohen 2022, 83.
180. Ibid., 83.
181. Ibid., 83; Moffett et al. 2019.
182. Adashi & Cohen 2022, 83; Levine 2019.
183. Kayentao, Ongoiba, Preston, et al. 2022.
184. Adashi & Cohen, 83.
185. Lederberg 1988, 359.
186. https://covid.cdc.gov/covid-data-tracker/#variant-proportions Accessed October 18, 2022.
187. Hachmann et al. 2022; cf. Qu et al. 2022.
188. For example, Qu et al. 2022.
189. Wang, Iketani, Li, et al. 2023.
190. Offit 2023.
191. Eyal & Gerhard 2022, 588; Adashi & Grupposo 2022.
192. Luo et al. 2022.
193. Fowles & Fields 2014; Frank, Keen, Rao, et al. 2022.

194. Fauci 2022.
195. Morens, Taubenberger, & Fauci 2021.
196. Lederberg 1988, 359; Postgate 2011; Clark 2008, 4.
197. Cf. Parfit 2011, volume 2, appendix J.
198. Finneron-Burns 2017; Ord 2020, 121–37.

References

Abbas, Abul, Lichtman, Andrew, and Pillai, Shiv. *Cellular and Molecular Immunology*, 9th ed. Amsterdam: Elsevier, 2018.

Adashi, Eli, and Cohen, Ivan Glenn. CRISPR Immunity: A Case Study for Justified Somatic Genetic Modification? *Journal of Medical Ethics* 48 (2022): 83–5.

Adashi, Eli, and Grupposo, Philip. SARS-CoV-2 Vaccines: The Mucosal Immunity Imperative. *Mayo Clinic Proceedings* 97 (2022): 1771–3.

Adler, Matthew, and Norheim, Ole (eds.). *Prioritarianism in Practice*. Cambridge: Cambridge University Press, 2022.

Alt, Frederick (ed.). *Advances in Immunology*, volume 146. Amsterdam: Elsevier/Academic Press, 2020.

American Society of Transplant Surgeons. Transplant Capacity in the COVID-19 Era and Early Vaccine Recommendations. https://asts.org/advoacy/covid-19-era.YEKAXI1Kgc8. Published December 3, 2020. Accessed November 19, 2022.

Anderson, Evan, Creech, Buddy, Berthaud, Vladimir, et al. Evaluation of mRNA-1273 Vaccine in Children 6 Months to 5 Years of Age. *New England Journal of Medicine* 387 (2022): 1673–87.

Anomaly, Jonathan. *Creating Future People: The Ethics of Genetic Enhancement*. New York: Routledge, 2020.

Arneson, Richard. Luck Egalitarianism Interpreted and Defended. *Philosophical Topics* 32 (2004): 1–20.

Arneson, Richard. *Prioritarianism*. Cambridge: Cambridge University Press, 2022.

Baker, Rebecca, Koroshetz, Walter, and Volkow, Nora. The Helping to End Addiction Long-Term (HEAL) Initiative of the National Institutes of Health. *Journal of the American Medical Association* 326 (2021): 1005–6.

Balu, Darrick T., and Coyle, Joseph T. Neuroplasticity Signalling Pathways Linked to the Pathophysiology of Schizophrenia. *Neuroscience and Biobehavioral Reviews* 35 (2011): 848–70.

Bao, Suqing, and Jiang, Xia. Anti-PD-1 Immune Checkpoint Inhibitor Inducing Endocrine Toxicity in a Patient with Advanced Lung Cancer: A Case Report and Literature Review. *Experimental and Theoretical Medicine* 24 (2022): 681. https://doi.10.3892/etm.2022.11617.

Baylis, Francoise. *Altered Inheritance: CRISPR and the Ethics of Human Genome Editing*. Cambridge, MA: Harvard University Press, 2019.

Beauchamp, Tom, and Childress, James. *Principles of Biomedical Ethics*, 8th ed. New York: Oxford University Press, 2019.

Beaver, Julia, and Pazdur, Richard. The Wild West of Checkpoint Inhibitor Development. *New England Journal of Medicine* 386 (2022): 1297–1301.

Bester, Johan C. *The Limits of Parental Authority: Childhood Wellbeing as a Social Good.* New York: Routledge, 2022.

Beurel, Eleonore, Toups, Marisa, and Nemeroff, Charles. The Bidirectional Relationship of Depression and Inflammation: Double Trouble. *Neuron* 107 (2020): 234–56.

Birnbaum, Rebecca, and Weinberger, Daniel. A Genetics Perspective on the Role of the (Neuro) Immune System in Schizophrenia. *Schizophrenia Research* 217 (2020): 105–13.

Blank, Christian, Haining, Nicholas, Held, Werner, et al. Defining "T-Cell Exhaustion." *Nature Reviews Immunology* 19 (2019): 665–74.

Bloomfield, Peter, Selvaraj, Sudhakar, Veronese, Mattia, et al. Microglial Activity in People at Ultra High Risk of Psychosis and in Schizophrenia: An[(11) C] PBR 28 PET Brain Imaging Study. *American Journal of Psychiatry* 173 (2016): 44–52.

Bluestone, Jeffrey, and Anderson, Mark. Tolerance in the Age of Immunotherapy. *New England Journal of Medicine* 383 (2020): 1156–66.

BMJ Conditions/Covid-19/Data Sewage. 378 (2022): o2007. https://doi:10 .1136/bmj.o2007. Published and accessed on August 11, 2022.

Boksa, Patricia. Abnormal Synaptic Pruning in Schizophrenia: Urban Myth or Reality? *Journal of Psychiatry and Neuroscience* 37 (2012): 75–7.

Bostrom, Nick, and Sandberg, Anders. Cognitive Enhancement: Methods, Ethics, Regulatory Challenges. *Science and Engineering Ethics.* 15 (2009): 311–41.

British Columbia Centres for Disease Control. www.bccdc.ca/health-info/dis eases-conditions/covid-19/data. Accessed September 14, 2022.

Brock, Dan. Priority to the Worse Off in Health Care Resource Prioritization. In Rosamond Rhodes, ed., *Medicine and Social Justice: Essays on the Distribution of Health Care*, 2nd edition. New York: Oxford University Press, 2012, 155–64.

Bullmore, Edward. *The Inflamed Mind: A Radical New Approach to Depression.* London: Short Books, 2018.

Burnet, Frank. *The Integrity of the Body: A Discussion of Modern Immunological Ideas.* Cambridge, MA: Harvard University Press, 1962.

CBC News. Alberta Court of Appeal Rejects Unvaccinated Woman's Request to Get Back on Transplant List. November 8, 2022. www.cbc.ca/news/canada/

edmonton/appeal-court-rejects-unvaccinated-woman-s-request-to-get-back-on-transplant-list. Accessed November 8, 2022.

Check, Erika. Gene Therapy: A Tragic Setback. *Nature* 420 (2002): 116–18.

Church, George, and Regis, Edward. *Regenesis: How Synthetic Biology Will Reinvent Nature and Ourselves*. New York: Basic Books, 2012.

Cifuentes-Rius, Ana, Desai, Anal, Yuen, Daniel, et al. Inducing Immune Tolerance with Dendritic-Cell-Targeting Nanomedicines. *Nature Nanotechnology* 16 (2021): 37–56.

Clark, William. *In Defense of Self: How the Immune System Really Works*. New York: Oxford University Press, 2008.

Cyranoski, David. CRISPR Gene Editing Tested in a Person for the First Time. *Nature* 539 (2016): 479.

Daniels, Norman. *Just Health: Meeting Health Needs Fairly*. New York: Cambridge University Press, 2008.

Dantzer, Robert. Neuroimmune Interactions: From the Brain to the Immune System and Vice Versa. *Physiological Reviews* 98 (2018): 477–504.

Dantzer, Robert, O'Connor, Jason, Freund, Gregory, et al. From Inflammation to Sickness and Depression: When the Immune System Subjugates the Brain. *Nature Reviews Neuroscience* 9 (2008): 46–56.

Doan, Thao, Melvold, Roger, and Waltenbaugh, Carl. *Concise Medical Immunology*. Philadelphia: Lippincott Williams & Wilkins, 2005.

Doudna, Jennifer, and Sternberg, Samuel. *A Crack in Creation: Gene Editing and the Unthinkable Power to Control Human Evolution*. New York: Houghton Mifflin Harcourt, 2018.

Driver, Julia. *Consequentialism*. New York: Routledge, 2012.

Eberl, Gerard. Immunity by Equilibrium. *Nature Reviews Immunology* 16 (2016): 524–32.

Edelstein, Michael, Abadi, Mohammed, and Wixon, Jo. Gene Therapy Clinical Trials Worldwide to 2007 – An Update. *Journal of Genetic Medicine* 9 (2007): 833–42.

Elisseeff, Jennifer, Badylak, Stephen, and Boeke, Jef. Immune and Genome Engineering as the Future of Transplantable Tissue. *New England Journal of Medicine* 385 (2021): 2451–62.

Emanuel, Ezekiel, Grady, Christine, Crouch, Robert, et al. (eds.) *The Oxford Textbook of Clinical Research Ethics*. New York: Oxford University Press, 2008.

Eyal, Nir. Why Challenge Trials of SARS-CoV-2 Vaccines Could Be Ethical Despite Risk of Severe Adverse Events. *Ethics & Human Research* 42 (2020): 24–34.

Eyal, Nir, Caplan, Arthur, and Plotkin, Stanley. Human Challenge Trials of Covid-19 Vaccines Still Have Much to Teach Us. *BMJ Opinion* January 8, 2021. https://blogs.bmj.com/bmj.2021/01/08/human-challenge-trials-of-covid-19-vaccines-still-have-much-to-teach-us/ Accessed November 19, 2022.

Eyal, Nir, and Gerhard, Tobias. Do Coronavirus Vaccine Challenge Trials Have a Distinctive Generalisability Problem? *Journal of Medical Ethics* 48 (2022): 107–9.

Fajgenbaum, David, and June, Carl. Cytokine Storm. *New England Journal of Medicine* 383 (2020): 2255–73.

Fauci, Anthony. It Ain't Over 'Till It's Over . . . But It's Never Over – Emerging and Re-emerging Infectious Diseases. *New England Journal of Medicine* 387 (2022): 2009–11.

Feinberg, Joel. The Child's Right to an Open Future. In *Freedom and Fulfillment: Philosophical Essays*. Princeton: Princeton University Press, 1992, 76–97.

Feinberg, Joel. *Harm to Others*. New York: Oxford University Press, 1986.

Finneron-Burns, Elizabeth. What's Wrong with Human Extinction? *Canadian Journal of Philosophy* 47 (2017): 327–43.

Fishman, Jay. Risks of Infectious Disease in Xenotransplantation. *New England Journal of Medicine* 387 (2022): 2258–67.

Fowles, Douglas, and Fields, Stanley. Deep Mutational Scanning: A New Style of Protein Science. *Nature Methods* 11 (2014): 801–7.

Francis, Thomas. On the Doctrine of Original Antigenic Sin. *Proceedings of the American Philosophical Society* 104 (1960): 572–8.

Frangoul, Haydar, Altshuler, David, Cappellini, Domenica, et al. CRISPR Cas9 Gene Editing for Sickle Cell Disease and Beta-Thalassemia. *New England Journal of Medicine* 384 (2021): 252–60.

Frank, Steven. *Immunology and the Evolution of Infectious Disease*. Princeton: Princeton University Press, 2002.

Frank, Filipp, Keen, Meredith, Rao, Anuradha, et al. Deep Mutational Scanning Identifies SARS-CoV-2 Nucleocapsid Escape Mutations of Currently Available Rapid Antigen Tests. *Cell* 185 (2022): 3603–16.

Gagnon, Alain, Miller, Matthew, Hallman, Stacey, et al. Age-Specific Mortality During the 1918 Influenza Pandemic: Unravelling the Mystery of High Young Adult Mortality. *PLOS ONE* 9 (2013): e69586. https://doi:10.1371/journal.pone.0069586.

Gagnon, Alain, Acosta, J. Enrique, Madrenas, Joaquin, et al. Is Antigenic Sin Always "Original?" Re-examining the Evidence Regarding Circulation of a Human H1 Influenza Virus Immediately Prior to the 1918 Spanish Flu.

PLOS Pathogens 11 (2015): e 1004615. https://doi:10.10371/journal .ppat.1004615.

Gauthier, David. *Morals by Agreement.* New York: Oxford University Press, 1986.

Glannon, Walter. Biomarkers in Psychiatric Disorders. *Cambridge Quarterly of Healthcare Ethics* 31: (2022): 444–452.

Green, Monica. The Four Black Deaths. *American Historical Review* 125 (2020): 1600–31.

Griffith, Bartley, Goerlich, Corbin, Singh, Avneesh, et al. Genetically Modified Porcine-to-Human Cardiac Xenotransplantation. *New England Journal of Medicine* 387 (2022): 35–44.

Guerriero, Jennifer. Macrophages: Their Untold Story in T Cell Activation and Function. *International Review of Cell and Molecular Biology* 342 (2019): 73–93.

Gumusay, Ozge, Callan, John, and Rugo, Hope. Immunotherapy Toxicity: Identification and Management. *Breast Cancer Research and Treatment* 192 (2022): 1–17.

Gyngell, Christopher, Douglas, Thomas, and Savulescu, Julian. The Ethics of Germline Gene Editing. *Journal of Applied Philosophy* 34 (2017): 498–513.

Gyngell, Christopher, Bowman-Smart, Hilary, and Savulescu, Julian. Moral Reasons to Edit the Human Genome: Picking Up from the Nuffield Report. *Journal of Medical Ethics* 45 (2019): 514–23.

Hacein-Bey-Albina, Salima, Garrigue, Alexandrine, Ward, Gary, et al. Insertional Oncogenesis in 4 Patients after Retrovirus-Mediated Gene Therapy of SCID-X1. *Journal of Clinical Investigation* 118 (2008): 3132–42.

Hachmann, Nicole, Miller, Jessica, Collier, Ai-Ris, et al. Neutralization Escape by SARS-CoV-2 Omicron Subvariants BA.2.12.1, BA.4, and BA.5. *New England Journal of Medicine* 387 (2022): 86–8.

Hall, Wayne, Carter, Adrian, and Forlini, Cythnia. The Brain Disease Model of Addiction: Is it Supported by the Evidence and Has it Delivered on Its Promises? *The Lancet Psychiatry* 2 (2015): 105–10.

Harris, John. *Enhancing Evolution: The Ethical Case for Making Better People.* Princeton: Princeton University Press, 2007.

He, Kaidi, Mack, Wendy, Neely, Michael, et al. Parental Perspectives on Immunizations: Impact of the Covid-19 Pandemic on Childhood Vaccine Hesitancy. *Journal of Community Health* 47 (2022): 39–52.

Hegle, Priti, and Chen, Daniel. Top 10 Challenges in Cancer Immunotherapy. *Immunity* 52 (2020): 17–35.

Hermann, Emilia, Lee, Benjamin, Balte, Pallavi, et al. Association of Symptoms after Covid-19 Vaccinations with Anti-SARS-CoV-2 Antibody

Response in the Framingham Heart Study. *JAMA NetW Open* 5 (2022): e223798. https://doi:10.1001/jamanetworkopen.2022.37908.

Heyman, Gene. *Addiction: A Disorder of Choice*. Cambridge, MA: Harvard University Press, 2009.

Hobbes, Thomas. *Leviathan*, ed. Christopher Brooke. London: Penguin, 1651/ 2017.

Howes, Oliver, and McCutcheon, Robert. Inflammation and the Neural Diathesis-Stress Hypothesis for Schizophrenia: A Reconceptualization. *Translational Psychiatry* 7 (2015): e2014. https://doi:10.1038/tp.2016.278.

Hsu, Patrick, Lander, Eric, and Zhang, Feng. Development and Application of CRISPR-Cas9 for Genome Engineering. *Cell* 157 (2014): 1262–78.

Huyghe, Leander, Van Parys, Alexander, Cauwels, Anje, et al. Safe Eradication of Large Established Tumors Using Neurovasculature-Targeted Tumor Necrosis Factor-Based Therapies. *EMBO Molecular Medicine* 12 (2020): e11223. https://doi:10.15252/emmm.201911223.

Inta, Dragos, Lang, Undine, Borgwardt, Stefan, et al. Microglia Activation and Schizophrenia: Lessons from the Effects of Minocycline on Postnatal Neurogenesis, Neuronal Survival and Synaptic Pruning. *Schizophrenia Bulletin* 43 (2017): 493–6.

Jacobson v. Massachusetts 197, US 11, 1905.

Janeway, Charles. The Immune System Evolved to Discriminate Infectious Nonself from Noninfectious Self. *Immunology Today* 13 (1992): 11–16.

Janeway, Charles. How the Immune System Protects the Host from Infection. *Microbes and Infection* 3 (2001): 1167–71.

Jinek, Martin, Chylinski, Krzysztof, Fonfara, Ines, et al. A Programmable Dual-RNA-Guided DNA Endonuclease in Adaptive Bacterial Immunity. *Science* 337 (2012): 816–21.

Johns Hopkins University Coronavirus Data. https://coronavirus.jhu.edu/data .mortality/adults/ https://coronavirus.juh.edu/data.mortality/children. Accessed January 2023.

Johnson, L. Syd. Xenotransplantation: Three Areas of Concern. *Hastings Bioethics Forum* January 19, 2022. www.thehastingscenter.org/xenotrans plantation-three-areas-of-concern/. Accessed November 17, 2022.

Johnson, L. Syd. Existing Ethical Tensions in Xenotransplantation. *Cambridge Quarterly of Healthcare Ethics* 31 (2022): 355–67.

Juengst, Eric. What Does Enhancement Mean? In Erik Parens, ed., *Enhancing Human Traits: Ethical and Social Implications*. Washington, DC.: Georgetown University Press, 1998, 29–47.

Kamm, Frances. *Intricate Ethics: Rights, Responsibilities, and Permissible Harm*. Oxford: Oxford University Press, 2007.

Kant, Immanuel. *Groundwork of the Metaphysics of Morals*, trans. H. J. Paton. New York: Harper & Row, 1785/1964.

Kayentao, Kassoum, Ongoiba, Aissata, Preston, Anne, et al. Safety and Efficacy of Monoclonal Antibody against Malaria in Mali. *New England Journal of Medicine* 387 (2022): 1833–42.

Keshavan, Matcheri, Giedd, Jay, Lau, Jennifer, et al. Changes in the Adolescent Brain and the Pathophysiology of Psychotic Disorders. *The Lancet Psychiatry* 1 (2014): 549–58.

Klein, Jan. *Immunology: The Science of Self-Nonself Discrimination.* New York: Wiley, 1982.

Klunk, Jennifer, Vilgalys, Taurus, Demeure, Christian, et al. Evolution of Immune Genes Is Associated with the Black Death. *Nature* 611 (2022): 312–19.

Koplin, Julian, Gyngell, Christopher, and Savulescu, Julian. Germline Gene Editing and the Precautionary Principle. *Bioethics* 34 (2020): 49–59.

Kraaijeveld, Steven, Gur-Arie, Rachel, and Jamrozik, Euzeblusz. Against COVID-19 Vaccination of Healthy Children. *Bioethics* 36 (2022): 687–98.

Lederberg, Joshua. Pandemics as a Natural Evolutionary Phenomenon. *Social Research* 55 (1988): 343–59.

Leng, Fangda, and Edison, Paul. Neuroinflammation and Microglial Activation in Alzheimer Disease: Where Do We Go From Here? *Nature Reviews Neurology* 17 (2021): 157–72.

Levine, Myron. Monoclonal Antibody Therapy for Ebola Virus Disease. *New England Journal of Medicine* 381 (2019): 2365–6.

Lin, Dan-Yu, Gu, Yu, Xu, Yangjianchen, et al. Effects of Vaccination and Previous Infection on Omicron Infections in Children. *New England Journal of Medicine* 387 (2022): 1141–3.

Lowe, Derek. Born CRISPRed: Now What? *Science Translational Medicine*, November 27, 2018. https://blogs.sciencemag.org/pipeline/archives/2018/11/27/born-crispred-now-what. Accessed November 24, 2022.

Luo, Sai, Zhang, Jun, Kreutzberger, Alex, et al. An Antibody from Single Human VH-Rearranging Mouse Neutralizes all SARS-CoV-2 Variants through Ba.5 by Inhibiting Membrane Fusion. *Science Immunology* 76 (2022): 5446. https://doi:10.1126/sciimmol.add5446. November 27, 2018. https://blogs.sciencemag.org/pipeline/archives/2018/11/27/born-crispred-now-what/.

Mantia, Charlene, and Buchbinder, Elizabeth. Immunotherapy Toxicity. *Hematology and Oncology Clinics of North America* 33 (2019): 275–90.

Mathews, Deborah, Fins, Joseph, and Racine, Eric. The Therapeutic "Mis"conception: An Examination of its Normative Assumptions and a Call for its Revision. *Cambridge Quarterly of Healthcare Ethics* 27 (2018): 154–62.

McHugh, R. Kathryn, Hearon, Bridget, and Otto, Michael. Cognitive-Behavioral Therapy for Substance Use Disorders. *Psychiatric Clinics of North America* 33 (2010): 511–25.

Melenhorst, Joseph, Chen, Gregory, Wang, Meng, et al. Decade-Long Leukemia Remission with Persistence of CD4+ CART Cells. *Nature* 602 (2022): 503–9.

Metzinger, Thomas, and Hildt, Elisabeth. Cognitive Enhancement. In Judy Illes and Barbara Sahakian, eds., *Oxford Handbook of Neuroethics*. Oxford: Oxford University Press, 2011, 245–64.

Miao, Lei, Zhang, Yu, and Huang, Leaf. mRNA Vaccine for Cancer Immunotherapy. *Molecular Cancer* 20 (2021): 41 https://doi:10.1186/s12943-021-01335-5.

Mill, John Stuart. 1859/1974. *On Liberty*, ed. Gertrude Himmelfarb. London: Penguin.

Miller, Andrew, Maletic, Vladimir, and Raison, Charles. Inflammation and its Discontents: The Role of Cytokines in the Pathophysiology of Major Depression. *Biological Psychiatry* 65 (2009): 732–41.

Miller, Andrew, and Raison, Charles. The Role of Inflammation in Depression: From Evolutionary Imperative to Modern Treatment Target. *Nature Reviews Immunology* 16 (2016): 22–34.

Mina, Michael, Kula, Tomasz, Leng, Yumei, et al. Measles Virus Infection Diminishes Preexisting Antibodies that Offer Protection from Other Pathogens. *Science* 366 (2019): 599–606.

Moffett, Howell, Harms, Carson, Fitzpatrick, Kristin, et al. B Cells Engineered to Express Pathogen-Specific Antibodies Protect Against Infection. *Science Immunology* 4 (2019): eaax0644. https://doi:10.1126/sciimmunol.aax0644.

Moran, Kate. *Kant's Ethics*. Cambridge: Cambridge University Press, 2022.

Morena, David, Taubenberger, Jeffrey, and Fauci, Anthony. Universal Coronavirus Vaccines – An Urgent Need. *New England Journal of Medicine* 386 (2021): 297–9.

Murphy, Caitlin, Walker, Adam, and Weikert, Cynthia Shannon. Neuroimflammation in Schizophrenia: The Role of Nuclear Factor Kappa B. *Translational Psychiatry* 11 (2021): 528. https://doi.10.1038/s41398-021-0167-0.

Muzio, Luca, Viotti, Alice, and Martino, Gianvito. Microglia in Neuroinflammation and Neurodegeneration. From Understanding to Therapy. *Frontiers in Neuroscience* 15 (2021): 742065. https://doi:10.3389/fnins.2021.742065.

Offit, Paul. Bivalent COVID-19 Vaccines – A Cautionary Tale. *New England Journal of Medicine*. 388 (2023): 481–3.

O'Neill, Onora. *Acting on Principle: An Essay on Kant's Ethics*, 2nd ed. Cambridge: Cambridge University Press, 2013.

Opel, Douglas, Diekema, Douglas, and Ross, Lainie Friedman. Should We Mandate a COVID-19 Vaccine for Children? *JAMA Pediatrics* 175 (2021): 125–6.

Ord, Toby. *The Precipice: Existential Risk and the Future of Humanity.* New York: Hachette Books, 2020.

Parent, Brendan, Caplan, Arthur, and Mehta, Sapna. Ethical Considerations Regarding COVID-19 Vaccination for Transplant Candidates and Recipients. *Clinical Transplantation* 35 (2021): e14421. https://doi.10.1111/ctr.14421.

Parfit, Derek. Equality and Priority. *Ratio* 10 (1997): 202–21.

Parfit, Derek. *On What Matters*, Volumes One and Two. Oxford: Clarendon Press, 2011.

Paus, Tomas, Keshavan, Matcheri, and Giedd, Jay. Why Do Many Psychiatric Disorders Emerge During Adolescence? *Nature Reviews Neuroscience* 9 (2008): 947–57.

Pereira, Marcus, Mohan, Sumit, Cohen, David, et al. COVID-19 in Solid Organ Transplant Recipients: Initial Report from the US Epicenter. *American Journal of Transplantation* 20 (2020): 1800–8.

Pradeu, Thomas. *The Limits of the Self: Immunology and Biological Identity.* New York: Oxford University Press, 2012.

Pradeu, Thomas. *Philosophy of Immunology.* Cambridge: Cambridge University Press, 2020.

Pravetoni, Marco, and Comer, Sandra. Development of Vaccines to Treat Opioid Use Disorders and Reduce Incidence of Overdose. *Neuropharmacology* 158 (2019): 107662. https://doi:10.1016/j.neuropharm.2019.06.001.

Pugh, Jonathan, Savulescu, Julian, Brown, Rebecca, and Wilkinson, Dominic. The Unnaturalistic Fallacy: Covid-19 Vaccine Mandates Should not Discriminate against Natural Immunity. *Journal of Medical Ethics* 48 (2022): 371–7.

Qu, Panke, Faraone, Julia, Evans, John, et al. Durability of Booster mRNA Vaccines against SARS-CoV-2 BA.2.12.1, BA.4, and BA.5 Subvariants. *New England Journal of Medicine* 387 (2022): 1329–31.

Rawls, John. *A Theory of Justice.* Cambridge, MA: Harvard University Press, 1971.

Reichenberg, Abraham. and Mollon, Josephine. Challenges and Opportunities in Studies of Cogition in the Prodrome to Psychosis: No Detail Is Too Small. *JAMA Psychiatry* 73 (2016): 1249–50.

Rogers, Jonathan, and Lewis, Glyn. Neuropsychiatric Sequelae of COVID-19: Long-Lasting but not Uniform. *The Lancet Psychiatry* 9 (2022): 762–3.

Rohaan, Maartje, Borch, Troels, van den Berg, Jost, et al. Tumor-Infiltrating Lymphocyte Therapy or Ipilimumab in Advanced Melanoma. *New England Journal of Medicine* 387 (2022): 2113–25.

Roltgen, Katharina, Nielsen, Sandra, Silva, Oscar, et al. Immune Imprinting, Breadth of Variant Recognition, and Germinal Center Response in SARS-CoV-2 Infection and Vaccination. *Cell* 185 (2022): 1025–40.

Rosenbaum, Lisa. The Future of Gene Editing – Toward Scientific and Social Consensus. *New England Journal of Medicine* 384 (2019): 971–5.

Rousseau, Jean-Jacques. *The Social Contract and Other Political Writings*, Victor Gourevitch trans. and ed. Cambridge: Cambridge University Press, 1762/1997.

Sauder, Colin, Allen, Luke, Baker, Elizabeth, et al. Effectiveness of KarXT (Xanomeline-Trospium) for Cognitive Impairment in Schizophrenia: Post Hoc Analyses from a Randomised, Double-Blind, Placebo-Controlled Phase 2 Study. *Translational Psychiatry* 12 (2022): 491. https://doi:10.1038/s41398 —22-02254-9.

Scanlon, Thomas. *What We Owe to Each Other*. Cambridge MA: Harvard University Press, 1998.

Scherer, Erin, Babikcr, Ahmed, Adelman, Max, et al. SARS-CoV-2 Evolution and Immune Escape in Immunocompromised Patients. *New England Journal of Medicine* 386 (2022): 2436–8.

Schietinger, Andrea. Turbocharging the T Cell to Fight Cancer. *New England Journal of Medicine* 386 (2022): 2334–6.

Schuman, Oliver, Robertson-Preidler, Joelle, and Bibler, Trevor. COVID-19 Vaccination Status Should Not Be Used in Triage Tie-Breaking. *Journal of Medical Ethics* 48 (2022).

Shaw, David. Vaccination Status and Intensive Care Unit Triage: Is it Fair to Give Unvaccinated COVID-19 Patients Equal Priority? *Bioethics* 36 (2022): 883–90.

Shiravand, Yavar, Khodadadi, Faezeh, Kashani, Seyyed, et al. Immune Checkpoint Inhibitors in Cancer Therapy. *Current Oncology* 29 (2022): 3044–60.

Silverman, Henry, and Odonkor, Patrick. Reevaluating the Ethical Issues in Porcine-to-Human Heart Xenotransplantation. *Hastings Center Report* 52 (2022): 32–42.

Sivan, Manoj, Greenhalgh, Trisha, Milne, Ruairidh, et al. Are Vaccines a Potential Treatment for Long COVID? *BMJ* 377 (2022):o988. Https://doi:10 .1136/bmj.o988.

Talbot, Sebastian, Foster, Simmie, and Woolf, Clifford. Neuroimmunology: Physiology and Pathology. *Annual Review of Immunology* 34 (2016): 421–47.

Tate, Warren, Walker, Max, Sweetman, Eiren, et al. Molecular Mechanisms of Neuroinflammation in ME/CFS and Long COVID to Sustain Disease and Promote Relapses. *Frontiers in Neurology* 13(2022): 877772. https://doi:10.3389/fneur.2022.877772.

Tauber, Alfred. *The Immune Self: Theory or Metaphor?* Cambridge: Cambridge University Press, 1994.

Tauber, Alfred. *Immunity: The Evolution of an Idea.* New York: Oxford University Press, 2017.

Thomson, Judith Jarvis. *The Realm of Rights.* Cambridge, MA: Harvard University Press, 1990.

Venkataramani, Varun, and Winkler, Frank. Cognitive Deficits in Long COVID-19. *New England Journal of Medicine* 387 (2022): 1813–15.

Vigo, Daniel, Thornicroft, Graham, and Atun, Rifat. Estimating the True Global Burden of Mental Illness. *The Lancet Psychiatry* 3 (2016): 171–8.

Volkow, Nora, and Li, Ting-Kai. Drug Addiction: The Neurobiology of Behavior Gone Awry. *Nature Reviews Neuroscience* 5 (2004): 963–70.

Volkow, Nora, Michaelides, Michael, and Baler, Ruben. The Neuroscience of Drug Reward and Addiction. *Physiological Reviews* 99 (2019): 2115–40.

Waltl, Inken, and Kalinke, Ulrich. Beneficial and Detrimental Functions of Microglia During Viral Encephalitis. *Trends in Neuroscience* 45 (2022): 158–70.

Wang, Qian, Iketani, Sho, Li, Zhiteng, et al. Alarming Antibody Evasion Properties of Rising SARS-CoV-2 BQ and XBB Subvariants. *Cell* 186 (2023): 1–8.

Wertheimer, Alan. *Coercion.* Princeton: Princeton University Press, 1987.

Wertheimer, Alan, and Miller, Franklin. There Are (STILL) No Coercive Offers. *Journal of Medical Ethics* 40 (2014): 592–3.

Wilkinson, Dominic. Liberty and the Child: Review of Bester, J. C. *The Limits of Parental Authority: Childhood Wellbeing as a Social Good. Bioethics* 36 (2022): 809–11.

Young, Michael, Sisti, Dominic, Rimon-Greenspan, Hila, et al. Immune to Addiction: The Ethical Dimensions of Vaccines against Substance Abuse. *Nature Immunology* 13 (2012): 521–4.

Acknowledgments

I am grateful to Thomasine Kushner, Syd Johnson, and Tom Buller for carefully reading and commenting on the manuscript. Thanks to Julia Ford, my Content Manager at Cambridge University Press. Special thanks to Teresa Yu for showing me the importance of the immune system in our lives

A modified version of "Figure 1–3. The Innate and Adaptive Immune Systems," from Thao Doan, Roger Melvold, and Carl Waltenbaugh, *Concise Medical Immunology,* Lippincott Williams & Wilkins 2005, p. 5, is used in Section 2 of this Element with permission from Wolters Kluwer Health, Inc.

A few paragraphs in Section 8 of this Element are from "Pathogens and Humans," *Hastings Bioethics Forum*, November 26, 2021, www.thehastingscen ter.org/humans-versus-pathogens/ and are used with permission from The Hastings Center.

Cambridge Elements ☰

Bioethics and Neuroethics

Thomasine Kushner
California Pacific Medical Center, San Francisco

Thomasine Kushner, PhD, is the founding Editor of the *Cambridge Quarterly of Healthcare Ethics* and coordinates the International Bioethics Retreat, where bioethicists share their current research projects, the Cambridge Consortium for Bioethics Education, a growing network of global bioethics educators, and the Cambridge-ICM Neuroethics Network, which provides a setting for leading brain scientists and ethicists to learn from each other.

About the series

Bioethics and neuroethics play pivotal roles in today's debates in philosophy, science, law, and health policy. With the rapid growth of scientific and technological advances, their importance will only increase. This series provides focused and comprehensive coverage in both disciplines consisting of foundational topics, current subjects under discussion and views toward future developments.

Cambridge Elements ≡

Bioethics and Neuroethics

Elements in the Series

Roles of Justice in Bioethics
Matti Hayry

The Ethics of Consciousness
Walter Glannon

Responsibility for Health
Sven Ove Hansson

Controlling Love: The Ethics and Desirability of Using 'Love Drugs'
Peter Herissone-Kelly

Immune Ethics
Walter Glannon

A full series listing is available at: www.cambridge.org/EBAN

Printed in the United States
by Baker & Taylor Publisher Services